Edexcel GCSE
Religious Studies

Unit 4
Religion and Life
Islam

Diane Spradbery

A PEARSON COMPANY

Published by Pearson Education Limited, a company incorporated in England and Wales, having its registered office at Edinburgh Gate, Harlow, Essex, CM20 2JE. Registered company number: 872828

www.pearsonschoolsandfecolleges.co.uk

Edexcel is a registered trade mark of Edexcel Limited

Text © Pearson Education Ltd 2009
First published 2009

14
10 9 8 7

British Library Cataloguing in Publication Data
A catalogue record for this book is available from the British Library.

ISBN 978 1 846904 22 6

Edited by Florence Production Ltd, Stoodleigh, Devon
Typeset by HL Studios, Long Hanborough, Oxford
Produced by Florence Production Ltd, Stoodleigh, Devon
Original illustrations © Pearson Education Ltd 2009
Illustrated by HL Studios, Long Hanborough, Oxford
Cover design by Pearson Education Ltd
Picture research by Zooid
Cover photo/illustration © blickwinkel/Alamy
Printed in Great Britain by Ashford Colour Press Ltd

Acknowledgements
The authors and publisher would like to thank the following individuals and organisations for permission to reproduce copyright material:

AFP/Getty Images/Cris Bouroncle, p. 85; akg-images, p. 16; BBC Photograph Library, p. 69; Burke Triolo Productions/Brand X Pictures, p. 10; dbimages/Alamy, p. 57; Design Pics Inc./Alamy, p. 10; Digital Vision, p. 21; Dinodia Images/Alamy, p. 11; Gavin Rodgers/Rex Features, p. 96; Image Source Black/Alamy, p. 13; Janine Wiedel/Photofusion Picture Library, p. 64; Jenny Matthews/Alamy, p. 61; John Birdsall MR/PA Photos, p. 64; Joseph Barrak/AFP/Getty Images, p. 45; Kazuyoshi Nomachi/Corbis UK Ltd, p.6; Kevin Carter/Megan Patricia Carter Trust/Sygma/Corbis UK Ltd, p. 40; Kick It Out, p. 81; Landov/PA Photos, p. 16; Leila Cutler/Alamy, p. 52; Lester Lefkowitz/Corbis UK Ltd., p. 28; Linographic, p. 10; Michael Boys/Corbis UK Ltd, p. 28; Mohamed Messara/Epa/Corbis UK Ltd, p. 86; Muslim Aid, pp. 42, 43; Nic Cleave Photography/Alamy, p. 36; Paul Glendell/Alamy, p. 16; Paul Grover/Rex Features, p. 16; Paul Prescott/Alamy, p. 54; Philip Game/Alamy, p. 75; ProLife Alliance, p. 35; Ronald Grant Archive, p. 30; Shutterstock, pp. 3, 9, 27, 32; Skyscan Photolibrary/Alamy, p. 62; Snap/Rex Features, p. 38; Stephane Cardinale/People Avenue/Corbis UK Ltd, p. 68; Steve Raymer/Asia Images RM/Photolibrary Group, p. 51; Ulrike Preuss/Photofusion Picture Library, p. 66; Yuri Samsonov/Shutterstock, p.8.

Permissions acknowledgements
The Holy Qur'an translation and commentary by A. Yusuf Ali. Used by permission of IPCI – Islamic Vision, Birmingham, UK.
p19 Ruqaiyyah Maqsood, *Examining Religions, Islam*, Heinemann 1995.
p43 Muslim Aid, http://www.muslimaid.org/index.php/what-we-do
p94 *Yorkshire Evening Post* 23 July 2007
p95 Chief Inspector of Schools cited in *The Times*, 18 January 2005

Websites
There are links to relevant websites in this book. In order to ensure that the links are up to date, that the links work, and that the sites are not inadvertently linked to sites that could be considered offensive, we have made the links available on the Pearson website at www.pearsonhotlinks.co.uk. When you access the site, the express code is 4226P.

Disclaimer
This Edexcel publication offers high-quality support for the delivery of Edexcel qualifications.
Edexcel endorsement does not mean that this material is essential to achieve any Edexcel qualification, nor does it mean that this is the only suitable material available to support any Edexcel qualification. No endorsed material will be used verbatim in setting any Edexcel examination and any resource lists produced by Edexcel shall include this and other appropriate texts.

Copies of official specifications for all Edexcel qualifications may be found on the Edexcel website – www.edexcel.com

Contents

Welcome to this Edexcel GCSE in Religious Studies Resource

These resources are appropriate for GCSE Religious Studies students on both the modular GCSE course certified in 2012 and 2013, and the linear GCSE course certified from 2014. Each Student Book covers one unit of the specification which makes up a Short Course qualification. Any two units from separate modules of the specification make up a Full Course qualification. Packed with exam tips and activities, these books include lots of engaging features to enthuse students and provide the range of support needed to make teaching and learning a success for all ability levels.

Features in this book

In each section you will find the following features:

- **an introductory spread** which introduces the topics and gives the Edexcel key terms and learning outcomes for the whole section

- **topic spreads** containing the following features:

  - **Learning outcomes** for the topic

  edexcel ⠿ key terms

  > **Key terms** are emboldened in the text, and definitions can be found in the glossary.

  ### Glossary

  Here we define other complex terms to help with understanding

  - **Activities** and **For discussion** panels provide stimulating tasks for the classroom and homework

  - a topic **Summary** captures the main learning points.

How to use this book

The book supports Edexcel Religious Studies Unit 4 Religion and Life based on a study of Islam. The book is split into the four sections of the specification and includes the key terms for each section and activities to help your understanding of the topics.

A dedicated suite of revision resources. We've broken down the six stages of revision to ensure that you are prepared every step of the way.

How to get into the perfect 'zone' for your revision.

Tips and advice on how to plan your revision effectively.

Revision activities and exam-style practice at the end of every section plus additional exam practice at the end of the book.

Last-minute advice for just before the exam.

An overview of what you will have to do in the exam, plus a chance to see what a real exam paper will look like.

What do you do after your exam? This section contains information on how to get your results and answers to frequently asked questions on what to do next.

ResultsPlus

These features help you to understand how to improve, with guidance on answering exam-style questions, tips on how to remember important concepts and how to avoid common pitfalls.

There are four different types of ResultsPlus features throughout this book:

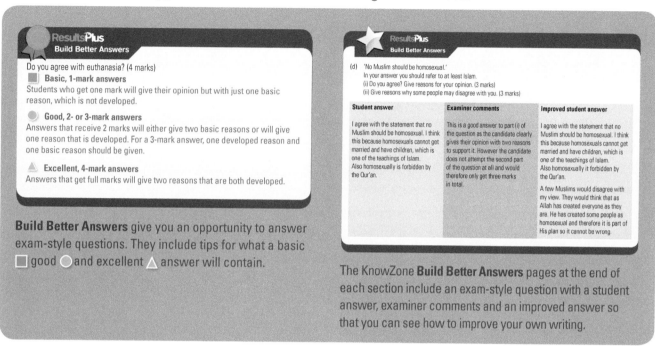

Build Better Answers give you an opportunity to answer exam-style questions. They include tips for what a basic ☐ good ◯ and excellent △ answer will contain.

The KnowZone **Build Better Answers** pages at the end of each section include an exam-style question with a student answer, examiner comments and an improved answer so that you can see how to improve your own writing.

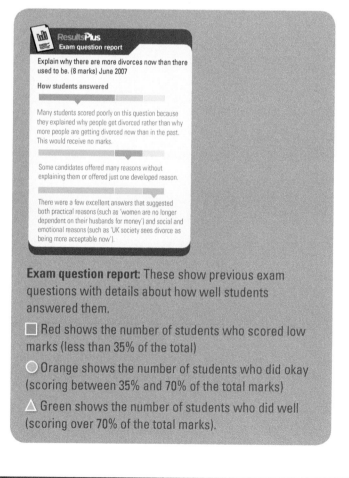

Exam question report: These show previous exam questions with details about how well students answered them.

☐ Red shows the number of students who scored low marks (less than 35% of the total)

◯ Orange shows the number of students who did okay (scoring between 35% and 70% of the total marks)

△ Green shows the number of students who did well (scoring over 70% of the total marks).

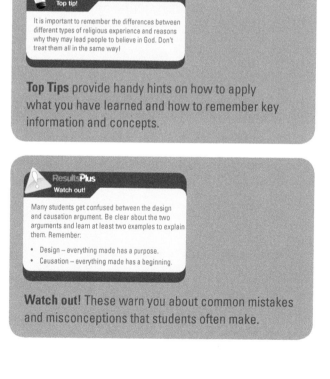

Top Tips provide handy hints on how to apply what you have learned and how to remember key information and concepts.

Watch out! These warn you about common mistakes and misconceptions that students often make.

Believing in Allah

Introduction

In this section you will consider and evaluate the reasons why some people believe in Allah and others do not. You will reflect on the questions raised by this belief and, by the end of the section, you will be able to express your own point of view using evidence to support your ideas.

You will learn what Muslims believe about Allah and how this belief relates to some of the big questions about life.

Learning outcomes for this section

By the end of this section you should be able to:

- give definitions of the key terms
- outline or describe the main features of a Muslim upbringing and how it might help people to believe in Allah
- outline or describe different explanations of the origins of the universe, including the 'causation', 'design' and scientific arguments
- explain why scientific explanations of the origins of the universe might cause some people to doubt Allah's existence and how Muslims respond to this
- outline or describe other examples of problems that may cause some people to doubt Allah's existence; for example unanswered prayer, and evil and suffering
- explain how Muslims respond to these arguments
- explain, with examples, how media programmes about religion may affect a person's attitude to belief in Allah
- evaluate why these programmes affect people's beliefs and whether this is fair to religious people
- express, with reasons and evidence, your own opinion about all these questions.

edexcel ::: key terms

agnosticism	free will	natural evil	omnipotent
atheism	miracle	numinous	omniscient
conversion	moral evil	omni-benevolent	prayer

Fascinating fact

It is estimated that there are 1.4 billion Muslims in the world. More than 1.6 million Muslims live in the UK, and roughly half of them live in London.

A kind old man

Superman

Non-existent

Invisible

Allah is…

A magician

All powerful

An angry judge

A woman

1 Scientists are still finding out about the incredible size and complexity of space. Discovering planets and stars that are hundreds of light years from earth. Discuss with a partner how far you think these wonders were made accidentally. Give reasons for your point of view.

2 Look at the diagram. Which comment is closest to your idea about Allah? Why?

1.1 Muslim upbringing and belief in Allah

Learning outcomes

By the end of this lesson you should be able to:

- describe a Muslim upbringing
- explain how a Muslim upbringing may lead to or support belief in Allah
- express your opinion about whether children should be made to follow their parents' religion.

Glossary

Aqiqa – Muslim naming ceremony when the baby's hair is shaved and its weight in gold or silver is given to charity.

Bismallah – The ceremony in some cultures when a Muslim child formally begins to learn about Islam.

Hadith – Sayings and actions of the prophet Muhammad as recorded by his family and friends.

Halal – That which is permitted or lawful.

Iqamah – The call to stand up for prayer.

Madrassah – Muslim school based at the mosque.

Salah – One of the five pillars of Islam. The five daily prayers.

How you are brought up shapes the person you become. The way adults around you treat you, the experience of the world you encounter, things you are told and introduced to all contribute to the person you are. This is known as your 'culture'.

Activities

1. Think about your own childhood and make a list of all the things that have made you who you are.
2. Use this list to create a poem that identifies what makes you the person you are. Look at the example below.

The family is a very important unit in Islam and there are many teachings about how to bring up children in both the Qur'an and Hadith. Muslims believe that the family was founded by Allah to give security and help to all its members. One of the purposes of a Muslim marriage is to have children and bring them up to be good Muslims. Muslim parents do this because they believe that this is the way Allah intended us to live and it gives meaning and purpose to life.

I am my older brother who first kicked a football at me

I am my granddad who first took me to a football match

I am my mother who loves me no matter what

I am my teacher who wants me to be successful

I am the teacher who first told me about God

ResultsPlus
Top tip!

The (b) questions in the exam will ask 'What do you think about…?'. Better answers include the reasons you give for holding this opinion. Be aware of the difference between just simply stating or describing what you think and actually giving the reasons why you think it!

4

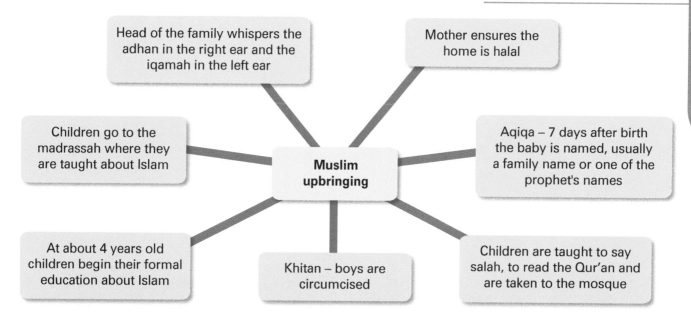

Head of the family whispers the adhan in the right ear and the iqamah in the left ear

Mother ensures the home is halal

Children go to the madrassah where they are taught about Islam

Muslim upbringing

Aqiqa – 7 days after birth the baby is named, usually a family name or one of the prophet's names

At about 4 years old children begin their formal education about Islam

Khitan – boys are circumcised

Children are taught to say salah, to read the Qur'an and are taken to the mosque

Activities

3 Look at the diagram on page 4. Consider each point and decide how it might help a child believe in Allah. Then link it with the phrases below:

- children learn by copying their parents so will believe Allah exists
- the child is born a Muslim and in time will take on the way of life required by Islam so will believe in Allah
- practising salah regularly reminds the child that Allah exists
- there are links with the traditions of Abraham, which are a sign of belonging to Allah
- names constantly remind the child that they are Muslim so Allah exists
- at about four years old children begin their formal education about Islam
- learning to read the Qur'an teaches the child about Allah
- mixing and learning with other Muslims helps to reinforce belief.

Activities

Challenge

Parents bring their children up to follow their religion because they think it is the best thing to do. They believe they have a responsibility to give their children the best life they can and for religious parents this means the child becoming a member of the parents' faith.

4 'Parents should not force their religion on their children'. How far do you agree with this statement?

For discussion

'Children under five are too young to learn about God.' Do you agree? Give reasons for your point of view.

Summary

- Muslim parents have a responsibility to teach their children about Islam.
- Muslim children begin their formal education about Islam after the bismillah ceremony.
- Living in a halal home, attending madrassah and learning about Islam are all part of a Muslim upbringing which leads to belief in Allah.

1.2 Religious experience and belief in Allah

Learning outcomes

By the end of this lesson you should be able to:

- say what a religious experience is and give examples
- describe a religious experience
- explain why a religious experience may lead to or support belief in Allah
- give your own opinion about religious experiences and give reasons for your opinion.

edexcel ⸬ key terms

Conversion – When your life is changed by giving yourself to Allah.

Miracle – Something that seems to break a law of science and makes you think only Allah could have done it.

Numinous – The feeling of the presence of something greater than you.

Some people who do not have a Muslim upbringing may come to believe in Allah for other reasons. Some people, although not Muslim, still have an association with Islam because of things such as:

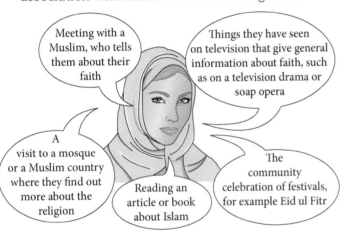

Meeting with a Muslim, who tells them about their faith

Things they have seen on television that give general information about faith, such as on a television drama or soap opera

A visit to a mosque or a Muslim country where they find out more about the religion

Reading an article or book about Islam

The community celebration of festivals, for example Eid ul Fitr

Glossary

Imam – A prayer leader and guide teacher about Islam.

Some people, when they are having a difficult time, may ask the imam for advice or pray to Allah for answers. If they believe Allah responds to them, they may come to a personal belief in Allah or it may strengthen their belief in Allah.

A religious experience is something that a person believes has brought them personally into direct contact with Allah. For Muslims, going on hajj (pilgrimage to Makkah) can be an intensely religious experience because they are aware of the presence of Allah especially when they stand on the plain of Arafat and seek forgiveness.

Pilgrims on hajj in Makkah.

The main religious experiences are:

Religious experience		How this leads to or supports belief in Allah
A **miracle**	This is something that happens which breaks the laws of science and people attribute to Allah.	People who have experienced a miracle are convinced that only Allah could have done this. This then provides them with the evidence that Allah exists and causes them to believe in Allah, or strengthens their belief in Allah.
An answered prayer	Prayer is the personal way that Muslims communicate with Allah. They may pray for guidance on how to live their life. An answered prayer is when the person praying believes that Allah has not only heard the prayer but has done as requested. For example, if someone is ill and prays to be better and then gets better.	This provides the person who prayed with the evidence that Allah exists (he must exist to have answered the prayer).
A **numinous** experience	This is when something completely astonishes you. It is such an experience that words are not enough to describe the feeling, but it leaves you feeling that something more powerful than you must exist. Often people refer to something in the natural world that is so beautiful that it overwhelms them, for example the view from a mountain top. For others it is something closer to home, such as the birth of a baby.	For some people this experience is so powerful it convinces them that Allah must exist.
A **conversion** experience	This is when someone who previously did not believe in Allah changes their belief and begins to believe Allah exists. A famous example is of the singer Cat Stevens, who converted to Islam and changed his name to Yusuf Islam. The person converted suddenly becomes aware of Allah and experiences a dramatic change of heart.	Conversion experiences often mean that a person is confronted with an ultimate choice whether or not to believe in Allah; it may be an event or someone else who confronts them. Whatever the event, the experience of conversion is a life-changing one.

Activities

1   Find out about the conversion of Cat Stevens. You could search on the Internet. What was it that made him give up his singing career to become a Muslim? Do you think this experience is common today?

2   Do you think Allah still does miracles today? Give reasons for your answer.

Summary

- Some people come to believe in Allah through miracles, answered prayers, a numinous experience or a conversion experience.
- These events and experiences bring believers into direct contact with Allah and therefore are used as evidence of Allah's existence.

1.3 The design argument and belief in Allah

8

Learning outcomes

By the end of this lesson you should be able to:

- outline the design argument
- explain how the natural world might lead someone to belief in Allah, or support belief in Allah
- explain, with reasons and examples, your own opinion on the design argument.

Activities

1 In your Design Technology department in school things are planned, designed and made. What was the most recent thing you designed and made? Describe the process you went through to create your masterpiece.

How would you feel if someone came along and said that the creation or making of your thing was just an accident and that you had had no contribution to it – it was just something that came together on its own?

Everyone has a unique fingerprint – no two people are the same. Compare the thumbprints of the people in your class – do you think this is design or chance?

What is design?

People have always enjoyed designing things. They have taken things and put them together in a variety of ways to come up with new objects either to make the world prettier or to make life easier. Designing things takes time and effort, plans are drawn up and ideas are made into reality. It is not often that something useful just happens by accident.

If we look at the design of the eye we see that it is made specifically for a purpose – seeing. If the lens of the eye is obscured then vision is impaired. Is the eye just a random collection of cells or has it been designed?

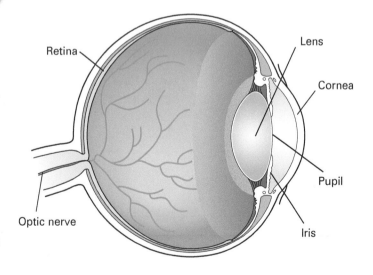

A cross-section through an eye.

Muslims believe that the world and the universe were designed, as everything works together for a purpose – to sustain life. They believe they did not come about just by accident or through a 'big bang', but were designed and made by Allah.

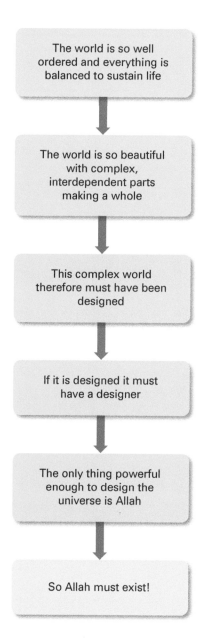

The world is so well ordered and everything is balanced to sustain life

↓

The world is so beautiful with complex, interdependent parts making a whole

↓

This complex world therefore must have been designed

↓

If it is designed it must have a designer

↓

The only thing powerful enough to design the universe is Allah

↓

So Allah must exist!

Paley's watch

A famous philosopher, William Paley, made an analogy between the world and a watch, as both have complex and distinctive features. He said that if someone found a watch (an old-fashioned watch with cogs and wheels inside) and had never seen one before in their lives they would be curious and amazed. They would naturally assume that something that was so carefully made and dependent on all the correct pieces being in the right place at the right time must have been designed and created by a very clever person.

Paley argued that the same could be said of the universe, which was much more complicated. It could never have happened by chance, it must have a clever designer and powerful creator. The only possible being capable of this is God. Therefore Paley concluded that God must exist.

Many people think that how scientists understand DNA is the most important discovery of the last hundred years. DNA was discovered, scientists did not create it, but they are amazed by it.

Activities

2 Do you think something as complex as DNA could have happened by accident?

3 If these accidents created life, why do we not see accidents today that create life or unique 'natural' happenings?

ResultsPlus
Watch out!

Make sure you link the argument from design with the existence of Allah.

Summary

- Some people argue the complex nature of the natural world and the uniqueness of a person's DNA and thumbprint support belief in Allah.

1.4 The causation argument and belief in Allah

Learning outcomes

By the end of this lesson you should be able to:

- outline reasons for believing in Allah based on the argument called causation
- explain how the argument for causation may or may not lead someone to believe in Allah
- express your own opinion about the strengths and weaknesses of this argument as reasons or evidence for believing in Allah.

Nothing in this world just happens by chance. A loaf of bread does not just end up in your house of its own accord. Like everything in life it has to begin with something – in this case a seed, which grows into wheat, is milled into flour and made into bread ready to be sold in a shop.

Many people would argue that the same is true of the universe. They argue that nothing happens by chance – everything has a reason or a cause. This is known as causation.

Activities

1 Can you give an example of something which happens that does not have a cause?

The argument follows a logical route.

> Nothing can happen by itself

↓

> Everything that happens has to be caused by something else

↓

> So the universe cannot have simply happened by itself

↓

> A very powerful force must have caused the universe as it is so great

↓

> Only Allah is great enough to be the cause

↓

> This means Allah must exist

The unmoved mover

A medieval thinker called Thomas Aquinas wrote:

> 'In the cosmos as we experience it, it is obvious to us that some things change. Now, whatever changes must be changed by another. And if that other itself changes then that too must be changed by another. But this cannot go on to infinity... you eventually have to arrive at something that is unchanging.
> This is God!'

A diamond is a natural stone made by carbon being compressed over hundreds of years. Diamonds are mined and then cut and polished to make beautiful jewellery. Can you trace the development of a diamond back to its source?

What Aquinas is saying is that eventually there has to be something which is the unmoved mover or first cause, and this has to be God. Islam has a similar argument for the existence of Allah, the Kalam argument.

The logic behind the causation argument appears to prove Allah's existence. However, the final step in the argument still requires belief in a superior being who caused the universe and some people find this hard to accept.

Activities

2   Look at the quote above and explain what Aquinas means in your own words.

3   What is your opinion about what he said? What are your reasons for saying this?

4   Explain how this argument could convince people to believe in Allah.

Activities

5   Make a list of reasons to agree with the causation argument (its strengths) and reasons to disagree with the argument (its weaknesses). What is your opinion on both sides of the argument and what reasons would you give to support your thoughts?

6   Work up these notes into a piece of writing that reflects both sides of the argument and concludes with your thoughts, with reasons.

ResultsPlus
Watch out!

Many students get confused between the design and causation argument. Be clear about the two arguments and learn at least two examples to explain them. Remember:

*   Design – everything made has a purpose.
*   Causation – everything made has a beginning.

Summary

*   Everything that exists has a cause.
*   The universe exists so it must have a cause.
*   The universe is so amazing the cause must be powerful.
*   The only unmade being powerful enough to make the universe is Allah.

1.5 Science and how it might cause non-belief in Allah

Learning outcomes

By the end of this lesson you should be able to:

- outline why some people do not believe in Allah
- describe the scientific explanation of the origins of the universe
- describe and explain the Muslim response to the scientific explanations of the universe
- explain why scientific explanations of the origins of the world may lead some people not to believe in Allah
- evaluate the different arguments given and express your own response to the scientific explanations of the universe, giving reasons and evidence for your opinion, showing you understand the alternative point of view.

edexcel ⠿ key terms

Agnosticism – Not being sure whether Allah exists.

Atheism – Believing that Allah does not exist.

The 'big bang'

In its simplest form, this is the idea that an explosion of matter took place about 15 billion years ago, and that from this explosion the universe came into being and that it continues to expand and evolve without any involvement from any outside power.

Activities

1 Make a chart with two columns, in the first column write a list of the reasons some people believe in Allah. Use the chapters you have already studied. In the second column give a reason why someone might not believe in Allah despite this evidence.

Reasons for believing in Allah	Alternative argument

People who do not believe in Allah are called atheists (this is **atheism**). Other people are unsure about what to believe and claim we cannot know if Allah exists or not, they are called agnostics (this is **agnostisicm**).

For people who do not believe in Allah there appear to be other explanations about how the world began (its origins). There are two main ideas which are linked together: the 'big bang' theory and the theory of evolution.

Evolution

Charles Darwin, after studying animals and insect life from different countries, came to the conclusion that all living things had changed to suit the environment in which they found themselves over a period of time. Each generation of animal therefore improved and evolved to survive.

According to modern scientists apes have common genetic material with human beings, indicating that humans evolved from apes. Darwin's theory suggests that Allah did not create all life uniquely but rather it evolved from one source.

A key reason that these theories lead some people to doubt Allah's existence is because they are supported by evidence that can be seen and tested. For example, fossils have been found which show the development of some animals into more complex forms. Scientists acknowledge that, at the moment, questions about the origin of the world cannot be totally explained by science, but claim that they will be in the future.

Muslim responses to scientific theories about the origins of the world

The Muslim starting point goes back before the beginning of the world because Allah existed before all things and all time. Allah existed before the creation of the world. Muslims believe that the Qur'an is the true and final word of Allah. In the Qur'an it says that Allah created the universe: therefore Muslims believe in creation not science. Muslims see the world as the manifestation of Allah's glory. They believe that Allah is in control of the whole universe and nothing happens within it without his knowledge.

Some Muslims believe that even if science can prove that the universe began with the 'big bang' then something must have caused the bang and that something was Allah. The world is so beautiful and mysterious that there must have been a power behind its beginning, and that must be Allah. It could not have happened randomly.

Activities

2   Create a wall display. On one side show the scientific answers to the origin of the world. On the other side add anything you can think of that could not have simply happened randomly. Next to each of your pictures put the reason for your choice (for example, next to a picture of a mountain scene, you might put the words 'too beautiful to have happened by chance').

Summary

- Scientific explanations of the origin of the world can lead people to doubt the existence of Allah.
- Muslims believe that the universe was created by Allah.
- Some Muslims believe that even if scientific theories are proved correct this does not mean that Allah did not begin the process.

1.6 Unanswered prayers and the Muslim response

14

edexcel key terms

Prayer – An attempt to contact Allah, usually through words.

Omni-benevolent – The belief that Allah is all-good.

Omnipotent – The belief that Allah is all-powerful.

Omniscient – The belief that Allah knows everything that has happened and everything that is going to happen.

Unanswered prayers – Can Allah hear? Does Allah listen? Does Allah care? Does Allah exist? Does Allah respond?

Atheists are confident that if Allah existed, and he was **omni-benevolent** and **omnipotent**, surely he would answer everyone's **prayers**. Many people experience suffering and pain in their own lives or watch as family and friends suffer, and Allah seems to do nothing. This makes it easy for some people to reject belief in Allah. They see millions of people praying for the same thing all over the world and nothing changes.

How do Muslims respond to this?

> Allah is omnipotent and sees the whole world not just our small part so will answer prayers that fit into Allah's plan for the world.

> Allah is **omniscient** and he knows what is best for us.

> This life is a test and not getting the answers we want to our prayers is part of that test.

> Allah is omni-benevolent and cares for us so sometimes the best answer is no.

Activities

1 Can you imagine being able to answer all the prayers that are made every day in the world – or even just in your school? In a small group, prepare a role-play to show what you think might happen if you said yes to all the prayers.

Muslims believe that Allah is in control and has a plan for everyone. Muslims pray every day for Allah to guide them through life so that they can serve him and become good Muslims. Muslims who do not trust in Allah because they have not got the answer they wanted to their prayer will have failed the test and will not go to Paradise.

Activities

2 Do you think prayer is a good way to deal with difficulties? Can you give an example of a prayer that was answered and made someone believe in Allah?

Activities

3 If Allah is omnipotent and knows what is best for you, is there any point in praying? Write a letter to a friend explaining what you think about prayer and in it give the reasons for your opinions as to whether Allah answers prayer or not.

ResultsPlus
Build better answers

'Unanswered prayers prove that Allah does not exist.'
In your answer you should refer to Islam.
(i)   Do you agree? Give reasons for your opinion.
      (3 marks)
(ii) Explain why some people might disagree with you.
      (3 marks)

Both parts of this question are worth 3 marks and will be marked in the same way

■ **Basic, 1-mark answers**
These answers will give one basic reason. Be aware of the difference between *saying* what you think, and *giving reasons* why you think it.

● **Good, 2-mark answers**
Answers that receive 2 marks will either give two reasons or will give one reason that is developed. One developed reason means you say something extra to explain your reason.

▲ **Excellent, 3-mark answers**
The answers either give three reasons, or two reasons with some explanation or evidence, or a fully-developed explanation of how the reasons support the opinion.

Summary

- Unanswered prayer can lead people to think that Allah does not exist.
- Muslims believe that unanswered prayer is part of life's test.

1.7 Evil and suffering and belief in Allah

Learning outcomes

By the end of this lesson you should be able to:

- explain what evil is and how this might cause suffering
- describe the problem of evil and suffering for Muslims
- explain why the existence of evil and suffering in the world might cause someone to doubt or reject belief in Allah.

edexcel ⠿ key terms

Natural evil – Things that cause suffering but have nothing to do with humans.

Moral evil – Actions done by humans that cause suffering.

There are two main types of evil: **natural evil** (suffering caused by nature), and **moral evil** (suffering caused by human beings).

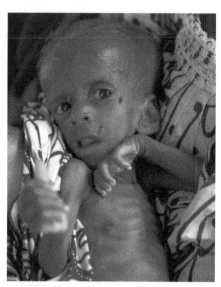

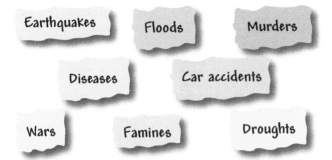

Earthquakes Floods Murders

Diseases Car accidents

Wars Famines Droughts

Activities

1   In the boxes above there are some things that cause suffering to people. Which ones are natural evil and which ones are moral evil? Do you think any of them could be both?

2   Study the pictures depicting evil and suffering. How do they make you feel? Explain why you reacted in this way?

Everyone experiences things in life that cause them to suffer, from stubbing your toe to watching a loved one die. This appears to be part of life. Many people link suffering and evil together, suffering is what happens after an act of evil.

Some people would say that the evidence of evil and suffering is the strongest argument against the existence of Allah. It can be outlined in this way.

If Allah is omniscient he would know how to remove the causes of suffering.

If Allah is benevolent he would not want people to suffer and would remove the causes of suffering.

Allah is… omni-benevolent, omnipotent, omniscient

If Allah is omnipotent he would be able to remove the causes of suffering.

Therefore as suffering and evil do exist EITHER Allah is not omnipotent, omniscient and omni-benevolent OR Allah does not exist.

Activities

3   Some people claim that there is no such thing as evil. It is just the absence of good. As darkness does not exist, it is just the absence of light. What do you think about this idea?

4   In many stories and films good and evil battle – good always wins. Why do you think this is so? Give some examples.

For discussion

Some people believe that suffering is necessary to remind us of good things. If we did not suffer we would not appreciate it when life is good. Do you agree with this idea? Does it make dealing with suffering easier or harder? Give reasons for your opinion.

ResultsPlus
Watch out!

Always read the question carefully. For example, in answer to the question 'Explain how evil and suffering may cause problems for some people', many candidates describe Muslim responses to evil and suffering. This is not what the question is asking – it is not asking why there is evil and suffering in the world. It is asking how evil and suffering can cause problems to people of faith. Therefore you need to explain how many people find it difficult to believe that Allah is benevolent because of suffering in the world.

Summary

- All people suffer in various different ways.
- Moral evil and natural evil are present in the world.
- The presence of evil and suffering in the world causes some people to doubt Allah's existence.

1.8 The Muslim response to evil and suffering

18

Learning outcomes

By the end of this lesson, you should be able to:

- describe and explain the Muslim response to evil and suffering
- evaluate the Muslim response giving your opinion with reasons.

In the last section we looked at the problem that evil and suffering can cause to religious people who believe that Allah is kind and powerful yet appears to be either unable or unwilling to stop suffering. This does not make sense and so some people use it as an argument against believing in Allah.

Muslims, however, believe in Allah who is all-powerful and in control of the universe and everything in it.

'God has the key of the unseen... He knows whatever is on land and in the sea; no leaf falls without His knowing it; there is not a grain in the darkness of the earth, or a green or dry thing, but it is carefully noted'. (Surah 6)

edexcel key terms

Free will – The idea that human beings are free to make their own choices.

Nothing happens without Allah's knowledge. This is not the same as saying that Allah can or cannot determine what happens. Muslims believe that Allah has commanded human beings to care for the world but has also given them **free will**, so how they use the world Allah created is their choice. However, Muslims also believe that they will be judged on the way they have used the world that Allah entrusted to them.

'On no soul does God place a burden greater than it can bear.' (Surah 2)

Muslims beleive that

Allah is...
Omnipotent
Omni-benevolent
Omniscient

Man can misuse his free will and cause suffering to others.

BUT

Life is a test and suffering is part of the test. Passing the test is rewarded after death.

Man can use his free will to help those who suffer.

Muslims believe that as humans we cannot possibly understand the reasons why things happen. Allah has a plan and a purpose for everyone and everything and we should trust that he knows what he is doing.

'On no soul does God place a burden greater than it can bear'. (Surah 2)

The following story illustrates this:

A poor man owned nothing but a fine white stallion. One day he found his paddock empty. 'What a terrible misfortune!' said his friends. 'Maybe yes, and maybe no,' he said.

The next day the stallion returned fetching with him five beautiful wild mares. 'What a wonderful fortune!' said his friends amazed. 'Maybe yes, and maybe no,' he said.

The next day his only son tried to tame a mare and was thrown down. He broke his legs and became a cripple. 'What a dreadful misfortune,' sighed his friends. 'Maybe yes and maybe no,' he replied.

The king came by and took away all the young men of the village to fight in the army – all except the cripple. The army lost and all the young men were killed…

Results Plus
Exam question report

Explain how Muslims respond to the problem of evil and suffering. (8 marks) June 2007

How students answered

Those answers which received low marks for this question tended to explain the problem of evil and suffering rather than explain how Muslims respond to it. They only gave one response that was not explained.

Many students did well on this question. Most explained one Muslim response to the problem of evil in depth, though some gave two brief responses.

There were quite a few excellent answers to this question which gave a detailed response to at least two of the different ways Muslims respond to the problem of evil and suffering.

For discussion

Do you think the belief that Allah allows evil in the world as part of a test would help people cope with their suffering better?

Activities

1 Make a table with three columns. In the first column write a list of difficulties people might face which cause them to suffer. In the second column, write down what you think a non-believer might say about each of the difficulties. And in the third column, write down what you think a Muslim might say about each of them.

2 Read the story about the man who owned the white stallion. Write a short paragraph explaining what you think it is saying about how Muslims respond to the problem of evil and suffering.

Summary

- Muslims believe that all suffering is part of the test in life. How you deal with the suffering will determine whether you are rewarded or punished after death by Allah.
- Muslims believe that Allah gave humans free will and some humans misuse that to cause suffering to others.
- Muslims believe Allah is all-powerful and in control so that any suffering will be part of his plan for the world.

1.9 The media and belief in Allah

Learning outcomes

By the end of this lesson you should be able to:

● describe two programmes that could affect a person's attitude towards belief in Allah

● explain how either of these programmes might affect a person's attitude towards belief in Allah

● evaluate messages sent through the media about believing in Allah and express your opinion about this, giving reasons and evidence.

For discussion

How do you think the media can influence the way people think about belief in Allah?

Television programmes

When viewers discuss a television programme, it can sound as if the characters are real and a part of their lives. People come to know them as if they were friends, and have a unique glimpse into their lives, sharing with them the joy and distress of the events that take place. This may be over a period of weeks with a soap opera on television or radio, or for a shorter time in the case of a television drama or film.

How much influence can the media have?

Television and films can influence our attitudes by presenting ideas as if they were facts, or facts as if they were fiction. When it comes to belief in a god, some programmes that are not specifically religious give a message to viewers that having faith and believing in a god is positive and should be embraced or encouraged, and that it can be beneficial. For example, the BBC4 programme *White Girl* gives a

very positive view of the Muslim family who help Leah. Their belief in Allah and the kindness they show to her make her want to share their beliefs. In the story *Leah*, the 'white girl' finds peace and safety within Islamic belief.

Some programmes on television present people who believe in a god as bizarre and slightly strange, and encourage the viewer to share this attitude. In the cartoon series *The Simpsons*, Ned, the Simpsons' neighbour, is often shown as bigoted and stupid.

There are many Islamic television channels which are designed to support belief in Allah and enable the viewer to feel part of the ummah, the worldwide brotherhood of Islam. These channels offer a wide variety of programmes ranging from news programmes to cartoon entertainment for children.

Life in Cold Blood *considers the amazing variety of creatures in the world.*

Activities

1 List the religious programmes you have watched on television or listened to (on the radio), and films you have seen that could affect a person's attitude towards belief in Allah.

2 Compare your list with a friend, and put the two lists together.

3 Choose two programmes from your combined list. Place them in the centre of a piece of paper. Around them, write the positive messages given by these programmes about belief in Allah and the negative messages given by these programmes about belief in Allah.

4 Programmes such as David Attenborough's *Life in Cold Blood* is about how life began. Identify any features from the film that might affect a person's belief in Allah. Make a list with two columns, one with those features that might encourage belief in Allah and one with those features that might discourage belief in Allah.

5 In your class debate the following statement taken from an exam question, considering the viewpoints both of people who agree with the statement, and those who disagree. You should say whether you agree or disagree, giving reasons for your opinions.

'*Religious programmes on television or the radio, or films encourage you to believe in Allah.*'

ResultsPlus
Top tip!

Remember, you must be able to discuss alternative points of view for the (d)-type questions in the exam. You will need either three reasons or two reasons which are explained, for both sides of the argument. You must refer to Islam in your answer to either d(i) or d(ii).

Summary

- Television, radio and films broadcast many scenarios that portray people believing in Allah.

- These can have both positive and negative effects on people's attitudes towards belief in Allah.

exam**zone**

KnowZone
Believing in Allah

Quick quiz

1 What is meant by **agnosticism**?

2 Give an example of someone who experienced a conversion to Islam.

3 Give the meaning of **omnipotent**.

4 Give an example of **moral evil**.

5 What is a **numinous** experience?

6 Do you think prayer solves problems? Give two reasons for your point of view.

7 What is **atheism**?

8 Give an example of a **miracle**.

9 Name one way a religious upbringing can help someone to believe in Allah.

10 What is meant by **causation**?

Plenary activity

1 Create a table of two columns that lists all the ways in which people come to believe in Allah and then explains how this leads to belief in Allah.

2 Create another table of three columns which lists:
a) reasons why people do not believe in Allah
b) why this has led them to reject belief in Allah
c) how a Muslim would respond to these reasons.

Find out more

Channel Four television shows many programmes that deal with key issues of religious belief, such as those described in this section. You could record some programmes and watch others. They will give you a better idea of how important religion is to people all over the world, whether they believe in Allah themselves or not.

Student tips

When I studied these topics for my GCSE I made sure that I knew all the key terms very well. This was so I could be sure of fully answering all the questions that asked for meanings of key terms but also so I could use some of them in other answers to show my understanding of the topics. For example, I used 'omnipotent' when writing about why Muslims have to find solutions to the problem of evil for the (c) question.

Self-evaluation checklist

Read through the following list and evaluate how well you know and understand each of the topics.
How well have you understood the topics in this section? In the first column of the table below use the following code to rate your understanding:

Green – I understand this fully.

Orange – I am confident I can answer most questions on this.

Red – I need to do a lot more work on this topic.

In the second and third columns you need to think about:

◗ Whether you have an opinion on this topic and could give reasons for that opinion, if asked.

◗ Whether you can give the opinion of someone who disagrees with you and give reasons for this alternative opinion.

Content covered	My understanding is red/orange/ green	Can I give my opinion?	Can I give an alternative opinion?
◗ How a Muslim upbringing encourages children to believe in Allah.			
◗ The nature of religious experience.			
◗ Different types of religious experience.			
◗ The design argument for the existence of Allah.			
◗ The argument for the existence of Allah, based on causation.			
◗ Why some people do not believe in Allah because they feel that science offers a better explanation for the origin of the world.			
◗ Some scientific explanations for the origin of the world.			
◗ Ways in which Muslims respond to scientific explanations for the origin of the world.			
◗ The nature of evil and suffering and why it is a problem for religious believers.			
◗ Muslim responses to the problem of evil and suffering.			
◗ The portrayal in the media of belief in Allah.			

examzone

KnowZone
Believing in Allah

Introduction

In the exam you will see a choice of two questions on this section. Each question will include four tasks, which test your knowledge, understanding and evaluation of the material covered. A 2-mark question will ask you to define a term; a 4-mark question will ask your opinion on a point of view; an 8-mark question will ask you to explain a particular belief or idea;

a 6-mark question will ask for your opinion on a point of view and ask you to consider an alternative point of view.

Choose the question you can answer best – remembering you need to answer all parts of the question you choose!

You must give your opinion, but make sure you do give two clear and properly thought-out reasons. These can be ones you have learned in class, even if they are not your own opinion. You mustn't use terms such as 'rubbish' or 'stupid' as these don't show that you are able to think things through carefully.

In your answer you should state whether or not you agree with the statement. You should also give reasons for your opinion.

In either (i) or (ii) you must refer to Islam.

Mini exam paper

(a) What is **atheism?** (2 marks)

(b) Do you think Allah is the cause of the universe?
Give **two** reasons for your point of view. (4 marks)

(c) Explain how a religious upbringing can lead to belief in Allah. (8 marks)

(d) 'Evil and suffering prove that Allah does not exist.'
In your answer you should refer to Islam.

(i) Do you agree? Give reasons for your opinion. (3 marks)

(ii) Explain why some people may disagree with you. (3 marks)

Here you need to give a short, accurate definition. You do not need to write more than one clear sentence.

The word 'explain' means you should give details of activities religious families may carry out together or ways in which they share their faith, but you must also show how these may lead to belief in Allah. This question is worth 8 marks so you must be prepared to spend some time answering it. You will also be assessed on your use of language in this question.

Now you have to give the opposite point of view, again using material you have learned during your studies. You don't have to say what you think about these alternative points of view, but you do need to show you understand why they are just as important to consider as your own opinion.

Mark scheme

(a) You can earn **2 marks** for a correct answer, and **1 mark** for a partially correct answer.

(b) To earn up to the full **4 marks** you need to give two reasons and develop them. Two brief reasons or only one developed reason will earn **2 marks**.

(c) You can earn **7–8 marks** by giving up to four reasons, but the fewer reasons you give, the more you must develop them. Because you are being assessed on use of language, you also need to take care to express your understanding in a clear style of English, and make some use of specialist vocabulary.

(d) To go beyond **3 marks** for the whole of this question you must refer to at least one religion. The more you are able to develop your reasons the more marks you will earn. Three simple reasons can earn you the same mark as one fully developed reason.

ResultsPlus
Build Better Answers

(b) Do you think Allah is the cause of the universe? Give **two** reasons for your point of view. (4 marks)

Student answer	Comments	Improved student answer
I think that Allah is the cause of the universe. The Qur'an and teachings of Muhammad tell us that Allah created the world and everything in it and I believe it.	The student has begun well by clearly stating their opinion as the question asks. They then give one reason why they believe this but do not really relate this to the argument for believing in Allah from causation. To improve the answer the student would need to write another reason or develop this reason more.	I think that Allah is the cause of the universe. The Qur'an and teachings of Muhammad tell us that Allah created the world and everything in it and I believe it. Everything in the world has a cause for its existence and the only thing powerful enough to have caused the universe is Allah.

Matters of life and death

Introduction

In this section you will learn about major issues that concern everybody, not just religious believers – those that address issues of life and death. We will all die at some point, but for religious believers what happens after death is crucially important, and also how we deal with life on Earth. How highly do we value life and what steps do we take to improve it and protect it? In this section you will learn how Muslims go about answering these questions.

Learning outcomes for this section

By the end of this section you should be able to:

- give definitions of the key terms
- explain why Muslims believe in life after death and how this belief affects the way they live their lives
- outline non-religious reasons for believing in life after death and why some people do not believe in life after death
- outline the current law on abortion in the United Kingdom, and explain why abortion is a controversial issue
- outline and explain different Muslim attitudes to abortion
- outline the current law on euthanasia in the United Kingdom, and explain why euthanasia is a controversial issue
- describe and explain Muslim attitudes to euthanasia
- describe the causes of world poverty
- explain how and why one Muslim agency is trying to end world poverty
- give arguments for and against the media being free to criticise what religions say about matters of life and death
- discuss how an issue raised in this section (abortion, euthanasia, life after death or poverty) has been presented in the media
- evaluate whether the treatment of this issue was fair to religious beliefs or religious people
- express your own point of view on these issues with reasons and evidence, considering other peoples' points of view.

edexcel ▦ key terms

abortion	barzakh	quality of life
akhirah	euthanasia	resurrection
al'Jannah	non-voluntary euthanasia	sanctity of life
assisted suicide	paranormal	voluntary euthanasia

Fascinating fact

In 2007 the abortion figures for the UK showed a rise of 2.5 per cent from 2006. The largest number of abortions were carried out on 19 year old women, whilst 4.4 per cent of abortions were carried out on girls under 16 and 19.8 per cent on girls under 18 years old. There have been 6.7 million legal abortions in the UK since 1967. (For more information, go to www.pearsonhotlinks.co.uk (express code 4226P) and click on the appropriate link.)

1 Work in pairs to answer these questions:
   - Is it ever right to kill?
   - When does life begin?
   - What happens when you die?

2 Look carefully at your answers. Write a list of questions that people might ask you to get you to provide reasons and evidence for your opinion.

   For example, if you said 'Life begins at birth', questions you might be asked are: When did the 'being' begin to have the potential of being a human being? Does this not make them alive? What is life? Is life given by Allah?

   Keep these questions and answers safe for the rest of the section to refer to when you are asked for your own opinion.

3 When we see new life, e.g. a baby, a kitten, a puppy, we know quite clearly that they are alive and precious. Think about some creatures we see that are not precious because they cause harm e.g. a rat. Make a list of any living thing, animal, human, plant that you think it is reasonable to kill. Put your reasons down as well.

2.1 Muslim belief in life after death

Learning outcomes

By the end of this lesson you should be able to:

- describe the different beliefs about life after death held by Muslims
- explain why there are different beliefs in life after death amongst Muslims
- explain why Muslims believe in life after death
- explain how these beliefs affect the way Muslims live their lives.

edexcel ⣿ key terms

Akhirah – Muslim beliefs about life after death.

al'Jannah – Heaven or Paradise (literally the garden).

Barzakh – The time of waiting between death and the Last Day.

Resurrection – The belief that, after death, the body stays in the grave until the end of the world, when it is raised.

Activities

1 Look at the pictures on this page. Consider what they say about life after death. Which picture is the closest representation of your own belief about life after death?

Create your own picture to express your feelings about death and the afterlife. It could be a symbolic collection of colours and words or just a simple drawing. Write a short explanation of how you came to choose this design.

All Muslims believe in **akhirah** – life after death. It is one of the main beliefs of Islam. Human life is divided into two parts, life on Earth and life after death, which is eternal. Life on Earth is a preparation for life after death. Muslims believe that life is a test and how you live your life determines what happens to you when you die. Everything that happens on Earth is decided by Allah and it is how you use your free will and react to it that matters.

Muslims also believe in the **resurrection** of the body. When people die, they stay in the grave until the last day (**barzakh**) when they will be raised to face Allah in Judgement. The good will go to **al'Jannah** (Paradise) and the bad will go to Hell. In the Qur'an Paradise is described as 'a garden under which rivers flow'. This implies that Paradise will be beautiful with sufficient water for all plants. Hell is often described as a place of fire.

The belief in life after death affects the way Muslims live their lives

- Muslims believe that they will be judged by Allah after death, so they live within the guidelines given in the Qur'an and Hadith.
- The belief that life is a test on which believers will be judged makes them want to do good.
- It offers comfort to those who have suffered the death of a loved one.

Some Muslims think that the paranormal is also evidence of life after death

The Qur'an teaches that there is life after death

Muhammad taught that there was life after death

'Do you think that we created you for nothing and that you would not be returned to us?' (Surah 23)

Why do Muslims believe in life after death

'... your good actions will benefit only you...' (Surah 41)

'In Paradise Allah prepares for the righteous believers what no eye has seen, no ear has heard and what the deepest mind could never imagine.' (Hadith)

The belief gives meaning and purpose to life

ResultsPlus
Build better answers

What is **resurrection**? (2 marks)

■ **Basic, 0-mark answers**
These answers will not address the question.

● **Good, 1-mark answers**
These answers will be partly correct.

▲ **Excellent, 2-mark answers**
These answers will give a short but full definition of what is meant by 'resurrection'.

Activities

2 Draw a chart with two columns. In one column write down some of the problems people face in life – for Muslims, part of the test – and in the other column write how dealing with the problem might help a person to pass the test and enter into Paradise.

3 Is it fair for a person's place in Heaven to be decided by what happens on Earth? Write down your answer to this question, giving your reasons.

Summary

- Life after death, akhirah, is one of the main beliefs in Islam.
- Belief in life after death affects how a Muslim lives every day.
- Muslims believe that Allah will judge everybody after death on how they have lived on Earth.

2.2 Non-religious belief in life after death

Learning outcomes

By the end of this lesson you should be able to:

- outline the reasons non-religious people believe in life after death
- evaluate the evidence presented and express your own point of view with reasons.

In the film Ghost *there is no religious reason given for life after death, although a lot of religious symbolism is used.*

For discussion

Is the portrayal of life after death in *Ghost* fair to religious beliefs and people? Is this an unfair picture of death? The medium explains why Sam Wheat is a ghost: she says that all ghosts are trapped souls, who have unfinished business. In this film the afterlife is a reward or punishment for the actions during life. Can this take place without Allah?

edexcel ⠿ key terms

Paranormal – Unexplained things that are thought to have spiritual causes, for example ghosts or mediums.

Glossary

Mediums – People who claim to be able to contact the dead.

Reincarnation – The belief that, after death, souls are reborn into another body.

Non-religious reasons for life after death

Many people who do not believe in Allah and consider themselves atheist or agnostic still believe in life after death. It appears that most people, religious or not, need to feel that life on Earth is not just all there is. There are three mains reasons that some people give for believing in some kind of existence after death.

Seeing ghosts

These are thought to be the spirits of dead people who for some reason have not travelled on to the next place. They can either be a physical presence that can be seen or a sense or feeling of someone being in room with you. It is believed some ghosts haunt the living, some come to support and look after loved ones and others try to contact the living.

Paranormal activities

Paranormal activities include, for example, contacting the spirits of the dead. People such as mediums claim to be able to contact the dead. Contacting the dead is forbidden in Islam. Many people attend seances and have found them convincing. Others claim they are the product of fraudsters who wish to take advantage of the grief of others.

Near-death experiences

These have been reported by patients who have been pronounced dead for a short time. They report leaving their bodies and seeing themselves from outside their body. In some cases they report seeing relatives and friends who have already died or a bright light they feel they want to travel towards. They are convinced this is evidence that there is an afterlife. An example of a near-death experience is shown below.

Activity

1 Carry out a survey of pupils and adults and find out how many of them believe in life after death. Create a spreadsheet that shows if they believe or not and what their reasons are – religious or non-religious.

For discussion

- Throughout human history many men and women have believed the existence of another life or world beside the one in which we are now living. Is there enough evidence to convince you that there is a parallel world?
- What do you think about the evidence of life after death from a non-religious point of view?
- Why do you think many people both religious and non-religious believe in some form of existence after death?

I don't remember being hit by the car. I do remember leaving the video shop with a DVD I'd rented and I was lying on the road, with someone (I think it must have been the driver of the car) saying that they'd called an ambulance. Soon after that I must have lost consciousness as it was like I was dreaming, but really realistically. I was walking along a path in the dark and couldn't see where I was going, I felt lost and afraid and kept turning round to try and see where I should go. It seemed to be getting darker and darker but then up ahead I could see a bright light and knew that I had to keep going towards that. When I got closer I could see people gesturing me to follow them. I just knew that one of them was my Dad who had died when I was young. I went from being scared to feeling very content and happy but then I felt a pull back to life. I woke up in a hospital bed with my wife beside me. The doctors told me later that they had had to resuscitate me – I had actually been dead for about four minutes.

Reincarnation

Reincarnation is the belief that a person's soul is reborn into another body when they die. This is often considered to be a religious reason for believing in life after death as it is believed by Hindus and Sikhs. However, many non-religious people also believe in reincarnation and think that it is just the moving on of the essence of a person from one body to another and does not involve a God or religion. Reasons given for believing this include experiences of déjà vu (the feeling of familiarity in a new situation) or memories of past lives.

Summary

- Many people believe that this life on Earth is not all there is to our existence.
- Some people base their belief in life after death on paranormal experiences such as seeing ghosts.

2.3 Non-belief in life after death

32

Learning outcomes

By the end of this lesson you should be able to:

● outline the reasons why some people do not believe in life after death

● evaluate the evidence presented and express your own point of view with reasons.

Many non-religious people do not believe in life after death in any form. Some of the reasons they give are the following.

● Life after death is simply impossible – we are either alive or dead.

● When a person dies their body decays, so how can they live again?

● There is no evidence for a life after death – no one has come back to tell us about it.

● Religion offers no good reasons to believe in an afterlife.

● Ideas of Heaven and Hell are simply made up to make us behave in this life or soften the fear of death.

● In an age when science explains the world, we should not believe in things that are unscientific.

● The scientist Richard Dawkins said that any belief in life after death was just superstition.

Activities

1 What would the following people say about Richard Dawkins' belief that life after death is just superstition?

I believe in Allah and therefore I think... because...

I do not believe in Allah and therefore I think... because...

Although, as we have seen, it is possible to believe in an afterlife without being religious, some non-believers think it is inconsistent to believe in an afterlife whilst rejecting other religious beliefs.

Belief in an afterlife requires us to imagine a state of affairs unlike this life because clearly our bodies no longer function. For many people this would be a pointless existence.

What do non-believers think happens after death?

Non-believers think that, as the body cannot function without the brain, there cannot be any life once the brain is dead. This is why when two doctors agree that a person on a life support machine is 'brain dead', they wish to turn the machine off as they think that there will not be any chance of the person living again.

Some people also think that a belief in life after death is just an idea to help us cope with someone we love dying because we hope to see them again in another life.

When we die our brain stops working and the body begins to decay. Philip Pullman, the children's author, has suggested that;

'What happens when we die is that we are sort of recycled. I mean, our bodies are clearly recycled and the different little bits, atoms, constituent parts, motes of dust that make up our consciousness, are also recycled. Nothing's lost.'

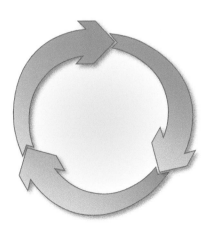

Activities

2 What do you think about life after death? Collect different points of view about what happens after death and create a graffiti wall of comments. Include your own view.

ResultsPlus
Build better answers

'Your soul will never die.'
In your answer you should refer to Islam.
(i) Do you agree? Give reasons for your opinion. (3 marks)
(ii) Explain why some people might disagree with you. (3 marks)

Both parts of this question are worth 3 marks and will be marked in the same way

■ **Basic, 1-mark answers**
These answers will give one basic reason. Be aware of the difference between saying what you think, and giving reasons why you think it.

● **Good, 2-mark answers**
Answers that receive two marks will either give two reasons or will give one reason that is developed. One developed reason means you say something extra to explain your reason.

▲ **Excellent, 3-mark answers**
The answers either give three reasons, or two reasons with some explanation or evidence, or a fully-developed explanation of how the reasons support the opinion.

Summary

- Many people do not believe in life after death as there is no scientific evidence to prove it exists.
- Many people do not believe in life after death because no one has returned from the dead to prove it exists.

2.4 The nature of abortion and abortion legislation

34

Learning outcomes

By the end of this lesson you should be able to:

- give a personal response to the questions 'When does life begin?' and 'Is it ever right to kill?'
- outline the current law on abortion and give a personal opinion, with reasons for it
- explain why abortion is a controversial issue
- outline the arguments for and against abortion.

The law

In the UK, **abortion** is only allowed if two doctors agree that:

- the mother's life is at risk
- the mother's physical or mental health is at risk
- the baby will be born severely handicapped
- there would be a serious effect on other children in the family.

Abortion is not allowed later than 24 weeks into the pregnancy.

The current law on abortion is based on the 1967 Abortion Act and the Human Fertilisation and Embryology Act of 1990. Before 1967 abortion was illegal in the UK.

Activities

1 Copy the timeline and add a cross showing where you think life begins. Your answer to this question will help you make decisions about the next few topics. Think about your reasons for choosing this point on the line, and write them down on the same piece of paper.

edexcel ⠿ key terms

Abortion – The removal of an embryo or foetus from the womb before it can survive.

Glossary

Embryo – The developing human during the first eight weeks after conception.

Foetus – The developing human from day 57 after conception to birth.

When does life begin?

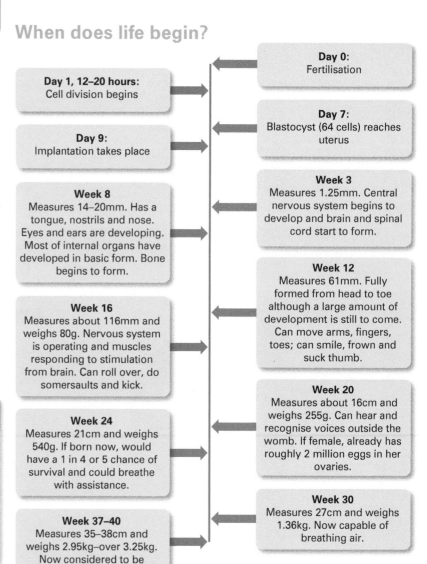

Day 0:
Fertilisation

Day 1, 12–20 hours:
Cell division begins

Day 7:
Blastocyst (64 cells) reaches uterus

Day 9:
Implantation takes place

Week 3
Measures 1.25mm. Central nervous system begins to develop and brain and spinal cord start to form.

Week 8
Measures 14–20mm. Has a tongue, nostrils and nose. Eyes and ears are developing. Most of internal organs have developed in basic form. Bone begins to form.

Week 12
Measures 61mm. Fully formed from head to toe although a large amount of development is still to come. Can move arms, fingers, toes; can smile, frown and suck thumb.

Week 16
Measures about 116mm and weighs 80g. Nervous system is operating and muscles responding to stimulation from brain. Can roll over, do somersaults and kick.

Week 20
Measures about 16cm and weighs 255g. Can hear and recognise voices outside the womb. If female, already has roughly 2 million eggs in her ovaries.

Week 24
Measures 21cm and weighs 540g. If born now, would have a 1 in 4 or 5 chance of survival and could breathe with assistance.

Week 30
Measures 27cm and weighs 1.36kg. Now capable of breathing air.

Week 37–40
Measures 35–38cm and weighs 2.95kg–over 3.25kg. Now considered to be full term.

Once we have established that something is alive, when would it be acceptable to end that life? Is it ever acceptable to take something away that you cannot replace?

The decision on whether abortion is right or wrong is based on the answers to these two questions. It is controversial because there are many different opinions on when life begins and if it is ever right to kill.

Some people think that abortion is acceptable. People who believe the mother should have the choice to have an abortion are called 'pro-choice':

- they argue that it is the woman's right to choose what happens to her own body

- they claim that abortion is the best option in certain situations, for example, if the child would be born with a severe disability or terminal illness, or if the mother's life is at risk if the pregnancy continues
- they argue that, in cases of rape, the child might be unwanted and cause both the mother and the child itself long-term mental problems
- they say there may be occasions when the mother might not be able to bring up a child for financial or emotional reasons (for example, a girl under the age of 16 may not be ready to be a mother).

Some people think abortion is unacceptable. People who believe the child has a right to life are called 'pro-life':

- they argue that life is special and should not be taken at any cost
- they believe life begins at conception, when the embryo has the potential of becoming a human being
- they argue that the unborn child should have the same human rights as any other human being
- they argue that loving parents could be found at the end of the pregnancy to provide a home for the child
- they argue that disabled children are no less important than able-bodied children and that they should have equal rights.

Summary

- People who believe life begins at conception are against abortion.
- People who believe life begins at birth will allow abortion in certain circumstances.

2.5 Different Muslim attitudes to abortion

Learning outcomes

By the end of this lesson you should be able to:

- give a definition of the sanctity of life
- outline the Muslim beliefs about abortion and the reasons for them
- explain why there are different attitudes to abortion within Islam.

Muslims believe that life is a gift from Allah. They believe life is holy and belongs to Allah and therefore only Allah has the right to take life away (this is the **sanctity of life**). Muslims believe that human beings have been made to serve Allah and are responsible for his Creation.

'We created Man from the essence of clay, We made out of that lump bones and clothed the bones with flesh.' (Surah 23)

'God gives you life and then causes you to die.' (Surah 45)

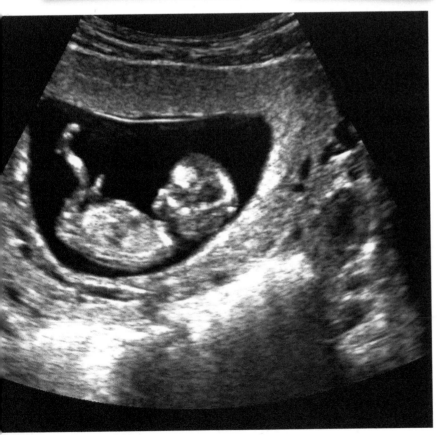

A scan showing a foetus at 12 weeks.

edexcel ⠿ key terms

Sanctity of life – The belief that life is holy and belongs to Allah.

There is also a verse in the Qur'an that says:

'Kill not your offspring for fear of poverty; it is we who provide for them and for you. Surely, killing them is a great sin.' (Surah 17)

So Muslims regard abortion as wrong. However, most Muslims allow it before 120 days, under certain circumstances, because in the Hadith it says that at 120 days *'an angel blows the breath of life into you'*, so the foetus becomes a living soul after this and as such should have the rights of all human beings.

- All schools of Muslim law accept that abortion is permitted if continuing the pregnancy would put the mother's life in real danger. The life of the mother is considered more important than that of the foetus and in this case abortion is the lesser of two evils. This is because the mother's life is important as she has responsibilities to the rest of the family and in many cases allowing the mother to die would also kill the foetus. This is the only reason accepted for abortion after 120 days of the pregnancy.
- Some Muslims will allow abortion before 120 days if there is something wrong with the foetus which means that it would not have a normal life.
- Other Muslims will allow abortion in cases of rape. It is reported that Bosnian women raped by the Serbian army were issued a fatwa allowing them to abort, but were urged to complete the abortion before 120 days.

Who...	... believes what	Why?
Most Muslims...	... are against abortion	• Life begins at conception and is a gift from Allah. • As life is a gift from Allah, only he can take it away. • Allah has a plan for every life and we should not interfere with that plan. • The teaching of the Qur'an is 'not to slay your children'.
Some Muslims...	... generally oppose abortion but allow it in some cases	• When the mother's life is at risk. They accept the idea of the 'lesser of two evils'.
Other Muslims...	... allow abortion	• In cases of rape, as Islam is a religion of compassion. • Modern technology allows the early detection of conditions and diseases that will cause suffering after the child is born. Abortions can be accepted to prevent suffering of the child later.

For discussion

What is the difference between killing a foetus before 120 days and a baby at 4 weeks after birth?

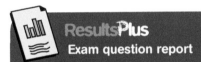

Results Plus
Exam question report

Explain why people argue about abortion. (8 marks) June 2007
How students answered

Most of the candidates who scored poorly on this question outlined Muslim views on abortion, which is not what the question is asking.

Many candidates could explain a few of the reasons why abortion is controversial but did not go into detail or explain the opposing view.

Most of the candidates who scored well on this question gave four developed reasons that explained the viewpoints of different people.

Activities

1 Write a letter to a problem page explaining that you are pregnant and are not sure what to do. You can make up the storyline yourself.

2 Swap your letter with a partner. Choose one of the Muslim viewpoints and reply to the letter.

3 Do you think the situation a person finds themselves in at any time gives them the right to kill? Write down three different examples, and then decide on your answers, giving your reasons.

4 Prepare and present a verbal presentation to your class about your point of view on abortion and how it differs or agrees with the views of most Muslims.

Summary

Most Muslims are against abortion as life is a gift from Allah, but some Muslims allow it in certain situations.

2.6 The nature of euthanasia and different Muslim attitudes

Learning outcomes

By the end of this lesson you should be able to:

● outline the law on euthanasia in the UK

● outline different Muslim attitudes to euthanasia

● explain why Muslims have these different views

● give your own opinions on these different views with reasons why you think this.

edexcel ⠿ key terms

Assisted suicide – Providing a seriously ill person with the means to commit suicide.

Euthanasia – The painless killing of someone dying from a painful disease.

Non-voluntary euthanasia – Ending someone's life painlessly when they are unable to ask, but you have good reason for thinking they would want you to do so.

Quality of life – The idea that life must have some benefits for it to be worth living.

Voluntary euthanasia – Ending life painlessly when someone in great pain asks for death.

Euthanasia is a Greek word that literally means 'good death'. More generally it is known as 'mercy killing'. There are several types of euthanasia and several ways in which it may be carried out.

- **Voluntary euthanasia** is when a person's life is deliberately ended at their request. Examples could be giving someone an injection that ends their life.
- **Assisted suicide** is the process of providing someone else with the means to end their life. An example could be buying the drugs for someone to take.
- **Non-voluntary euthanasia** is when a person's life is deliberately ended when the person is unable to communicate their wishes but when it is believed that it is what they would have wanted.

In all these cases the person who wishes to die must be in great pain and/or dying.

- Active euthanasia is carried out by a doctor performing a deliberate action, such as an injection.
- Passive euthanasia is carried out when medical treatment is not given or is stopped.

The law

Euthanasia in any form is currently illegal in Britain. Doctors may switch off a life-support machine with the agreement of the relatives if the patient is clinically dead with no hope of recovery.

Activities

In the film Whose Life is it Anyway? *Ken Harrison is an artist who makes sculptures. One day he is involved in a car accident, and is paralysed from his neck down. All he can do is talk, and he wants to*  *die. In hospital he makes friends with some of the staff, and they support him when he goes to trial to be allowed to die. He argues a strong case for the right to die.*

1 Look at the photograph showing Richard Dreyfuss as Ken. Do you think people should be allowed to choose how and when they die? Why? Write down your thoughts about this, giving your reasons.

2 Make a list of any other films, television dramas or soap operas that you can recall where they have explored the issue of euthanasia. Do you think the media represents the beliefs of religious people fairly? Give reasons for your comments.

Most Muslims object to euthanasia because it goes against the principle of the sanctity of life.

Who...	... believes what	Why?
Most Muslims...	... are against euthanasia	• Allah created human beings so only he has the power to take away their life. • The Qur'an bans suicide and euthanasia is a form of suicide. • Terminally ill patients can still worship Allah. • Euthanasia could be used for evil purposes. • Life is a test from Allah that determines the afterlife. • Euthanasia is cheating the test.
Some Muslims...	... allow the turning off of a life-support machine	• Some Muslim scholars have agreed that a life-support machine may be turned off when there are no signs of life, as the life has already ended.

Some people who agree with euthanasia may use the argument that Allah intends that humans should have a good **quality of life**. This means that they should be able to do the things that are meaningful to them and make them feel good about life. However, Muslims, believe that everything that happens to them is part of Allah's will and part of his test, and that poor quality of life is caused by poor reaction to the test and not an excuse to shorten the test.

Keeping people alive with expensive drugs is not a good use of NHS resources

Everyone has a right to choose how they end their life

If euthanasia was legalised many problems might arise

Everyone should be able to choose to die with dignity

Build better answers

Do you agree with euthanasia? (4 marks)

■ **Basic, 1-mark answers**
Students who get one mark will give their opinion but with just one basic reason, which is not developed.

● **Good, 2- or 3-mark answers**
Answers that receive 2 marks will either give two basic reasons or will give one reason that is developed. For a 3-mark answer, one developed reason and one basic reason should be given.

▲ **Excellent, 4-mark answers**
Answers that get full marks will give two reasons that are both developed.

Activities

3 What do you think about euthanasia? Prepare a short presentation for your class showing the reasons for and against euthanasia, giving both your point of view and the Muslim point of view. Give reasons for both viewpoints.

Summary

• Muslims are strongly opposed to euthanasia on the grounds that life is a gift from Allah and no one has the right to take it away.

• Some Muslims will allow a life-support machine to be switched off.

2.7 The causes of world poverty

Learning outcomes

By the end of this lesson you should be able to:

- outline the causes of world poverty
- describe the work of one Muslim agency to try to end world poverty.

Glossary

LEDC – Less economically developed country.

ResultsPlus
Watch out!

There are many causes of world poverty. In the exam some candidates spend too much time criticising the developed countries rather than focusing on the different causes of poverty and how the suffering could be reduced.

Activities

1 Look at this picture. What questions does it raise in your mind about matters of life and death? What feelings and emotions do you have when you look at this? Why?

Activities

2 Look at the diagram of the causes of world poverty. Which of these causes of poverty are man-made problems?

3 In your own words, outline the causes of world poverty.

4 How far can these causes be relieved by charities as well as by government action?

Most people accept that in the UK we live in a developed country. We have the resources we need to have a long life, a good standard of living, and a good quality of life. Those countries which do not have the resources to provide what is needed for a long life and a good standard of living are called less developed or less economically developed countries (LEDCs). Some countries are at an in-between stage and are considered to be 'developing' countries.

There are many things that contribute to world poverty; they may not be the same in each country and some causes contribute to others.

Natural disasters
Many LEDCs are in areas where there are regular natural disasters, for example earthquakes and floods, which can destroy homes, farmland, etc.

Lack of health care and education
Lack of clean water, too many children, lack of education, AIDS/HIV, etc. – all prevent the country from developing.

War
Many LEDCs suffer from wars. Wars destroy crops, homes, schools and hospitals and create refugees. A neighbouring country can often move from developing to less developed when war refugees arrive needing shelter, food, etc.

Corrupt leaders
Some governments are corrupt and aid from other countries does not always reach the people who need it.

Causes of world poverty

Cash crops
Many poor countries try to solve their financial problems by growing cash crops (for example, cotton, tea, coffee, etc.) to sell to the more economically developed countries, but this uses land that could be used to grow food for their own people, leading to starvation.

Debt
All LEDCs suffer from debt. They have to borrow money from banks in developed countries and pay large amounts of interest to the bank, using money that they could have spent on development. Many LEDCs try to get money from abroad by growing and selling crops. But the rich countries pay their own farmers grants (subsidies) to grow crops and put high taxes on the crops from LEDCs so the LEDCs' goods are expensive. The rich countries then export the crops their own farmers have grown at prices lower than the LEDCs can grow them for.

How can the causes of poverty be removed?

- Richer countries reducing debts by charging less interest or cancelling the debt completely.
- Helping the country provide good education and skills so people can get jobs and become self-sufficient.
- Give training in health care so that people understand the need for clean water and use protection against AIDS/HIV.
- Help in emergency situations, e.g. earthquakes.

Activities

Challenge
If you used the argument that abortion or euthanasia could be justified on the grounds of the person not having a good quality of life, where does this leave the people in less developed countries, or those living in poverty in Britain?

Summary

- There are a number of different causes of world poverty.
- Many of the causes of poverty are linked together, making it hard for countries to develop.

2.8 How and why one Muslim agency is trying to end world poverty

42

Learning outcomes

By the end of this lesson you should be able to:

- explain why Muslims work to try to end world poverty
- describe the work of one Muslim agency aiming to end world poverty
- explain the reasons why the agency does this work
- evaluate the work of the agency giving reasons for your point of view.

The Qur'an says that a truly righteous person 'gives food for the love of Him, to the needy, the orphan, the prisoner of war (saying): "We feed you only for the sake of Allah."' (Surah 76).

Why should Muslims help people in need?

Muslims believe that Allah has created everyone as equals and therefore no one should be rich at the expense of others.

Muhammad said:

> '... he is not a believer who eats his fill while his neighbour remains hungry by his side.' (Hadith)

Care and compassion for others is part of showing one's love for Allah. Apart from zakah, the compulsory charitable tax that they give once a year, Muslims are encouraged to give more to charity in the form of sadaqah. This is a voluntary gift that a Muslim might give in response to hearing about someone in need. If a Muslim hears about a problem and does nothing about it they are ignoring the true meaning of being a member of the worldwide brotherhood of Islam, the ummah.

Muhammad also said:

> '... an ignorant person who is generous is nearer to Allah than a mean person who is full of prayer.' (Hadith)

For discussion

How can someone who prays a lot not be close to Allah? What do you think Muhammad meant?

Glossary

Ummah – The worldwide Muslim community.

What do Muslims do to help relieve world poverty?

Some Muslims have set up organisations that work to relieve world poverty. Muslim Aid is one such charity. It is based in the UK but works internationally to help save and improve the lives of people.

Muslim Aid providing disaster relief.

Assalamu alaykum – Peace and blessing be upon you

Search: [search...] [Go]

WHAT WE DO   **GET INVOLVED**   **ABOUT US**   **MEDIA CENTRE**

Working in over 70 countries across Africa, Asia and Europe, Muslim Aid is striving to help the poor overcome the suffering endured due to natural disasters and lack of life's basic necessities.

We work with all in need, regardless of their race, religion, gender, nationality or political opinion.

Whilst responding to emergencies is one of our major priorities, we also work on strategic programmes to eliminate poverty that focus upon:

- Education
- Skills training
- Provision of clean water
- Healthcare
- Income generation projects.

These projects ensure that individuals can have access to basic necessities and the skills necessary to generate an income so that they are not permanently dependent on aid agencies for food and shelter.

[Adapted from the Muslim Aid website www.muslimaid.org/index.php/what-we-do.]

ResultsPlus
Build Better Answers

Choose one Muslim agency and explain why it works to relieve poverty. (8 marks)

Basic, 1- to 2-mark answers
These answers will give an example of a Muslim agency but may describe the work of this agency rather than focus on why it does that work.

Good, 3- to 6-mark answers
These answers will give some reasons.

Excellent, 7- to 8-mark answers
These answers will give an example of an agency and will usually give four developed reasons why it does that work. Alternatively, answers may give two reasons but explain them fully.

Activity

1 Carry out a piece of research into one Muslim development agency and investigate the work done by them, and see how this relates to their Muslim beliefs. Many organisations have websites and information that they will share with you.

After your research, create a leaflet or poster to advertise the work of the agency you choose to investigate and give reasons why Muslims should support this.

Summary

Many Muslims work to end world poverty because it is part of showing their love for Allah.

2.9 Matters of life and death in the media

Learning outcomes

By the end of this lesson you should be able to:

- explain how different forms of media tackle matters of life and death
- understand how they reflect a range of different views on life and death issues
- offer your own opinion on how the media deal with these matters and assess how your views may be different to others.

ResultsPlus
Watch out!

There are many programmes on the television that cover the issues of death, life after death, abortion, euthanasia and poverty. You may study some with your teacher and all of these will be good examples to use in your answers to the GCSE questions. However, always read the question carefully – in the past many students have just described a media programme rather than answering the question!

Why is it important that these issues are explored in the media?

It is important that matters of life and death, including abortion and euthanasia, are explored and discussed in the media because:

- issues of life and death affect everyone
- people have very strong feelings about these issues
- opinions are very divided and it is important we know how people think
- controversial issues need to be discussed openly
- people have the right to know about developments in these issues
- people need to know how the law may change.

There are several forms of media that allow these issues to be presented to the public.

- *Newspapers*: they have different styles of presentation and can indicate their own opinions on issues and possible changes in the law.
- *Radio*: many radio shows, including some plays, feature matters of life and death.
- *Television news*: matters of life and death are prominent on the television news, but like other forms of media the stories are selected and presented from a particular point of view.
- *Television documentaries*: they offer the opportunity to focus on major issues at length, identifying different positions on the same issue.
- *Soap operas*: they use ongoing storylines to examine issues in depth in a way that is accessible to the general public.

- *Television dramas*: they may specifically focus on matters of life and death.
- *Situation comedies*: the main aim of these programmes is to make people laugh but because they take place in everyday situations and audiences can relate to the characters, these programmes often feature matters of life and death.
- *Cartoons*: in the same way as situation comedies, these may deal with matters of life and death, even those that are aimed at children.
- *Films*: they might use a detailed plot to examine an issue in depth, often based on a novel that has already introduced this idea.

Activities

1. (a) Have a look at this week's newspapers. Make a list of how many stories there are about matters of life and death.

   (b) In the same way, watch the television news. Explain how it deals with issues of life and death.

   (c) Are there any differences between the two? Give reasons.

Soap operas

Soap operas are long-running serials concerned with everyday life in which several storylines are carried over from one episode to the next. Regular events in soap operas include issues of family and relationships, but also issues such as abortion, euthanasia and dealing with illness and death. If a particularly emotional issue has been addressed by a soap, then a helpline phone number is often displayed at the end, so people who have been affected by the issues raised can get support or extra information.

Films and documentaries

A surprising number of films are made that tackle matters of life and death. In most cases the moral theme of a film is presented alongside the more usual themes of popular film – romance, family dramas, adventures or fantasy – because most films are designed to entertain as well as inform.

There are many useful documentaries on television that cover issues of life and death such as rare illnesses or disabilities, or the cases of individuals who have to make difficult choices. These may not reach such a wide public audience as a film because they do not set out to entertain but to inform.

Activities

2 Choose one type of media. Outline a report or a storyline that covers death, abortion, euthanasia or poverty. Explain how the issue was dealt with. Present this work as a spider diagram, putting the issue in the middle and adding the different opinions expressed in the programme or newspaper.

- Did the writers present all sides of the argument?
- Was a religious response to the issue covered?
- If not, why do you think this was missed out?
- If it was covered, was it a fair portrayal of religious people's beliefs?

3 Look at the photograph below, which was taken soon after a terrorist bombing in Beirut, Lebanon in 2007.

- Should newspapers and television show such pictures – or should they be censored first? Give your reasons.
- What considerations need to be taken before a newspaper prints a story/picture concerning a tragic death? Why?

For discussion

1 Do you think different rules of censorship, sensitivity and good taste apply to films and documentaries than the rules for newspapers?

2 Even in feature films the director may make a choice to focus the whole film on a moral issue. Think about how they do this and whether viewers leave the film thinking differently about an issue. Should the director convey his beliefs, or should he present a whole range of opinions on an issue for us to discuss and consider?

Activities

4 Write a short review of a film you have seen that dealt with matters of life and death. Give your opinion on how well or badly the subject was treated and whether it was accurate and fair.

5 'There should be no news censorship. Television and newspapers should show things exactly as they happen.' Do you agree? Give reasons for your view.

Summary

- A wide range of media can be used to present matters of life and death to a wide audience.
- Newspapers and television news, soap operas, documentaries and films all present issues to the public.

KnowZone
Matters of life and death

Quick quiz

In the following table match the words with their correct meaning. Try doing it without looking up the words in the Student Book or a dictionary.

Word	Meaning
Abortion	The idea that life must have some benefits for it to be worth living
Akhirah	Ending life painlessly when someone in great pain asks for death
Al'Jannah	Muslim beliefs about life after death
Assisted suicide	The time between death and the last day
Barzakh	The painless killing of someone dying from a painful disease
Euthanasia	Providing a seriously ill person with the means to commit suicide
Non-voluntary euthanasia	Heaven or Paradise
Paranormal	Unexplained things that are thought to have spiritual causes, e.g. ghosts
Quality of life	The removal of the embryo or foetus from the womb before it can survive
Resurrection	The belief that life is holy and belongs to Allah
Sanctity of life	Ending someone's life painlessly when they are unable to ask, but you have good reason for thinking they would want you to do so
Voluntary euthanasia	The belief that after death the body stays in the grave until the end of the world when it is raised

Student tips

There are a lot of controversial topics in this section. It is important not to say 'All Muslims believe...' unless you are absolutely sure that this is right! For many of these topics Muslims hold a variety of views so it's better to use phrases such as 'Most Muslims believe...' or 'A few Muslims think...'

Self-evaluation checklist

Read through the following list and evaluate how well you know and understand each of the topics.
How well have you understood the topics in this section? In the first column of the table below use the following code to rate your understanding:

Green – I understand this fully.

Orange – I am confident I can answer most questions on this.

Red – I need to do a lot more work on this topic.

In the second and third columns you need to think about:

- Whether you have an opinion on this topic and could give reasons for that opinion, if asked.
- Whether you can give the opinion of someone who disagrees with you and give reasons for this alternative opinion.

Content covered	My understanding is red/orange/green	Can I give my opinion?	Can I give an alternative opinion?
Explain why Muslims believe in life after death.			
Show how this belief affects the way they live their lives.			
Outline non-religious reasons for believing in life after death and why some people do not believe in life after death.			
Outline the law on abortion and explain Muslim attitudes to abortion.			
Outline the law on euthanasia in the United Kingdom, and explain why euthanasia is a controversial issue.			
Describe and explain Muslim attitudes to euthanasia.			
Describe the causes of world poverty.			
Explain how and why one Muslim agency is trying to end world poverty.			
Evaluate whether the media are fair in their reporting of religious beliefs or their portrayal of religious people.			
Explain why Muslims believe in life after death.			
Show how this belief affects the way they live their lives.			

examzone

KnowZone
Matters of life and death

Introduction

In the exam you will see a choice of two questions on this section. Each question will include four tasks, which test your knowledge, understanding and evaluation of the material covered. A 2-mark question will ask you to define a term; a 4-mark question will ask your opinion on a point of view; an 8-mark question will ask you to explain a particular belief or idea;

a 6-mark question will ask for your opinion on a point of view and ask you to consider an alternative point of view.

Choose the question you can answer best – remembering you need to answer all parts of the question you choose!

Mini exam paper

(a) What is **non-voluntary euthanasia?** (2 marks)

(b) Do you agree with euthanasia?

Give **two** reasons for your point of view. (4 marks)

(c) Explain why most Muslims do not agree with abortion. (8 marks)

(d) 'The paranormal proves that there is life after death.' In your answer you should refer to Islam.

(i) Do you agree? Give reasons for your opinion. (3 marks)

(ii) Give reasons why some people may disagree with you. (3 marks)

You must give your opinion, but make sure you do give two clear and properly thought-out reasons. These can be ones you have learned in class, even if they are not your own opinion. You mustn't use terms such as 'rubbish' or 'stupid' as these don't show that you are able to think things through carefully.

In your answer you should state whether or not you agree with the statement. You should also give reasons for your opinion.

In either (i) or (ii) you must refer to Islam.

Here you need to give a short, accurate definition. You do not need to write more than one clear sentence.

The word 'explain' means you should give details of activities religious families may carry out together or ways in which they share their faith, but you must also show how these may lead to belief in Allah. This question is worth 8 marks so you must be prepared to spend some time answering it. You will also be assessed on your use of language in this question.

Now you have to give the opposite point of view, again using material you have learned during your studies. You don't have to say what you think about these alternative points of view, but you do need to show you understand why they are just as important to consider as your own opinion.

Mark scheme

(a) You can earn **2 marks** for a correct answer, and **1 mark** for a partially correct answer.

(b) To earn up to the full **4 marks** you need to give two reasons and develop them. Two brief reasons or only one developed reason will earn **2 marks**.

(c) You can earn **7–8 marks** by giving up to four reasons, but the fewer reasons you give, the more you must develop them. Because you are being assessed on use of language, you also need to take care to express your understanding in a clear style of English, and make some use of specialist vocabulary.

(d) To go beyond **3 marks** for the whole of this question you must refer to at least one religion. The more you are able to develop your reasons the more marks you will earn. Three simple reasons can earn you the same mark as one fully developed reason.

Results Plus

Build Better Answers

(c) Explain why most Muslims do not agree with abortion. (8 marks)

Student answer	Comments	Improved student answer
Muslims believe that life is a gift from Allah. Some Muslims believe that life begins at conception and therefore they would always disagree with abortion as it would be destroying something that Allah has created. Other Muslims do not believe that life begins until 120 days after conception and they would allow abortion in some situations, such as after rape, before this date.	The student begins well by correctly stating that Muslims believe that life is a gift from Allah and therefore some Muslims would disagree with abortion because of this but this could have been made clearer. Then the student continues by explaining a reason why some Muslims do agree with abortion in certain circumstances, which is not answering the question. To answer more fully the candidate needs to go into much more depth or give more reasons why some Muslims disagree with abortion.	Muslims believe that life is a gift from Allah. Some Muslims believe that life begins at conception and therefore they would always disagree with abortion as it would be destroying something that Allah has created. Muslims believe in the sanctity of life, which means that abortions should never be allowed. Some Muslims also disagree with abortion because it teaches in the Qur'an 'not to kill your children' and they would class abortion as murder. Another reason is that Muslims believe that Allah has a plan for every living thing and to kill a foetus would interfere with Allah's plan and would therefore be wrong.

Marriage and the family

Introduction

In this section you will learn about the attitudes and beliefs of Muslims towards sex outside marriage, marriage, and divorce. You will consider changing attitudes to these topics. You will learn about Muslim attitudes to contraception and homosexuality. You will evaluate the alternative points of view on these topics and come to a personal conclusion with reasons to support it.

Learning outcomes for this section

By the end of this section you will be able to:

- give definitions of the key terms
- outline the changes in attitudes in the UK to sex outside marriage, marriage, divorce, family life and homosexuality and give reasons for these
- describe different Muslim attitudes to sex outside marriage, explain why there are different attitudes and express your own point of view with reasons
- explain the purpose of marriage in Islam and how this is shown through the wedding ceremony
- describe and explain the different attitudes of Muslims to homosexuality and express your own point of view with reasons
- outline the Muslim teachings on family life and its importance
- describe how mosques help with the upbringing of children and explain how this helps keep the family together
- outline different methods of contraception and Muslim attitudes towards them
- evaluate, with examples, how these topics have been covered in the media.

edexcel ::: key terms

adultery	contraception	mahr	procreation
civil partnership	contract	nuclear family	promiscuity
cohabitation	homosexuality	pre-marital sex	re-constituted family

Think of all your family – grandparents, aunts, uncles, cousins, etc. – who live with you, near you or far away from you. Draw a series of circles with yourself in the middle, your closest family in the next, etc.

ME

Now look at your diagram and work out what type of family you live in.

For example, if all your family live in the same house or the same street (or very nearby), you are in an extended family. If most of them live away, you are in a nuclear family. If it is just you and your mum or dad you are in a single-parent family.

Fascinating fact

There are 17.1 million families now living in the UK. The UK has the highest number of single-parent families in Europe.

3.1 Changing attitudes towards marriage, divorce, family and homosexuality in the UK

Learning outcomes

By the end of this lesson you should be able to:

- describe and explain the changing attitudes in the UK towards marriage, divorce, family life and homosexuality
- suggest possible reasons for the changes in attitude and comment on them.

edexcel ::: key terms

Civil partnership – A legal ceremony giving a homosexual couple the same legal rights as a husband and wife.

Cohabitation – Living together without being married.

Homosexuality – Sexual attraction to a person of the same sex.

Glossary

Divorce – The legal termination of a marriage.

Marriage – Where a man and a woman are legally united for the purpose of living together as a couple.

WHAT HAS CHANGED?

1. Divorce is very common.
2. More couples **cohabit**.
3. More single-parent families.
4. Many same sex couples now have **civil partnerships**.
5. Now most people view divorce, cohabitation and homosexuality as acceptable.

Families are changing. Families in the UK have changed over the last 50 years – with more single-parent and step families, changes in economic well-being, and decreasing family size.

In the UK, attitudes towards marriage, divorce, the family and **homosexuality** have also changed in recent years. Changes in attitude towards things like this take time and often occur without being noticed for a while. Our society now accepts more things that are different and were not considered the acceptable 'norm' thirty years ago.

Why are there changes?

- People are less willing to put up with bad treatment from their partners
- Divorce is quick and often inexpensive
- Divorce does not carry the social stigma that it did in the past
- People are less religious and do not feel bound to their marriage vows
- Laws regarding divorce have changed
- Social welfare helps single parents
- It is illegal to treat anyone differently due to their colour, age or sex
- Society sees diversity as a good and interesting part of life

Many people think that some of these changes are not a good thing and have made the world an unhappier place.

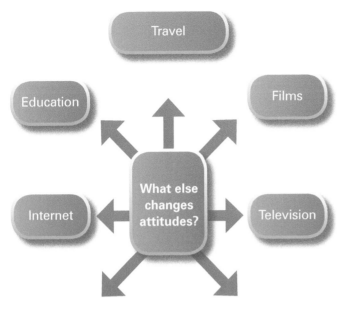

Activities

2 (a) Is change always a good thing? Make two lists – one of good changes and one of bad changes.

(b) Next to each one give the reason why you think it is either good or bad.

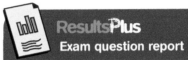

ResultsPlus

Exam question report

Explain why there are more divorces now than there used to be. (8 marks) June 2007

How students answered

Many students scored poorly on this question because they explained why people get divorced rather than why more people are getting divorced now than in the past. This would receive no marks.

Some candidates offered many reasons without explaining them or offered just one developed reason.

There were a few excellent answers that suggested both practical reasons (such as 'women are no longer dependent on their husbands for money') and social and emotional reasons (such as 'UK society sees divorce as being more acceptable now').

Activities

1 Look at the diagram above. For each item, give an example of the way the particular thing has changed attitudes, e.g. celebrities – Elton John having a civil partnership ceremony.

Discuss the possible answers that would complete the following chart and then draw and complete your own copy.

Area of change	What has changed	Evidence of change
Attitude to sex outside marriage		
Attitude to cohabiting		
Attitude to divorce		
Attitude to homosexuality	e.g. same-sex relationships are more easily accepted	The introduction of civil partnerships

Summary

- Attitudes to marriage, divorce, family and homosexuality have changed a great deal in recent years.
- Some believe this is a good thing as it gives people more freedom and choice.
- Others think that change is a bad thing and a decline of traditional and religious values and eventually unhappiness.

3.2 Muslim attitudes to sex outside marriage and homosexuality

54

Learning outcomes

By the end of this lesson you should be able to:

- describe and explain the attitudes of Muslims to sex outside marriage
- evaluate the teaching of Islam about sex outside marriage
- understand and explain different Muslim attitudes to homosexuality
- evaluate these opinions and state with reasons your own point of view.

edexcel key terms

Adultery – A sexual act between a married person and someone other than their marriage partner.

Pre-marital sex – Sex before marriage.

Procreation – Making a new life.

Promiscuity – Having sex with a number of partners without commitment.

'When a husband and wife share intimacy it is rewarded and is a blessing from Allah: just as they would be punished if they engaged in illicit sex.' (Hadith)

All Muslims believe marriage is the right place for sex. They condemn sex before marriage (**pre-marital sex**), extra-marital sex (**adultery**) and sex between people of the same gender (homosexuality).

Islam is against any kind of intimacy between couples who are not married to each other. This is why Muslim teenagers do not go out together or attend social events unless they have adults with them. This protects both sexes from doing anything that is against the will of Allah.

'Let no man be in privacy with a woman who is not lawful unto him or shaytan will be the third.' (Hadith)

Men and women are instructed in the Qur'an to dress modestly so that they will be known for their faith not for their looks. Muslims believe that modest clothing also helps to prevent them thinking about sexual matters or tempting others to think about sexual matters.

Muslims believe that sex is an important part of being human but that sexual relationships should only take place between married couples as part of a committed relationship. In the Qur'an it says:

'The things that my Lord has indeed forbidden are shameful deeds whether open or secret.' (Surah 7)

Activities

1. How far do you think it is true that modest clothing prevents Muslims thinking about sexual matters? Discuss your ideas with a partner.
2. Do you think it would be right for a Western female tourist to wear a sleeveless top and shorts when holidaying in a Muslim country? Give reasons for your opinion.

All Muslims believe that **promiscuity** is wrong because they believe that sexual freedom outside marriage leads to problems in society. Adultery causes many marriages to go wrong, sexually-transmitted diseases increase and many people, especially young adults, suffer emotional upheavals when relationships break down.

In Islam the family is the most important unit and nothing should be allowed to undermine it.

Pre-marital sex   Homosexuality   Cohabitation

Sex outside marriage   ← Adultery

Forbidden and should be punished according to the Qur'an

It is common in UK society for couples to cohabit (live together) without being married. Many see this as a way of preparing for marriage. They argue that if you love someone then it makes sense to share everything with them, even sex.

Activities

3   On television, in films and in books there are many cases of couples cohabiting. Choose a story you have seen or read about and explain why the couple chose to live together outside marriage.

For discussion

Do you think that forbidding sex before marriage is out of date? Give reasons for your point of view.

Muslim attitudes towards homosexuality

Attitudes to homosexuality have also changed in society; same-sex couples are often seen on television, for example on *Coronation Street*. Many famous people in government and show business have civil partnerships.

Islam condemns all forms of sex that take place outside marriage. This includes sex between same-sex couples.

Allah made human beings for the purpose of **procreation** and same-sex relationships cannot do that, so they are not fulfilling the purpose for which they were made. Muslims regard homosexuality as a worse sin than adultery and some believe it should be punished by death.

Their belief is based on the story of Lut (Lot) who lived in a city where homosexuality was common. Allah condemned and burnt the city, killing all the inhabitants, but saved Lut and his family because he was a righteous man.

Most Muslims believe that we all have choices to make regarding our sexuality. Those who choose a same-sex relationship are going against the teaching of the Qur'an.

'Of all the creatures in the world, will you approach males and abandon those whom Allah created for you as mates.' (Surah 26)

However there are verses that state that if homosexuals repent and ask for forgiveness then Allah will accept them.

Activities

4   Prepare a speech for debate 'As everyone is created by Allah they cannot choose their sexual orientation.' First decide whether your speech will agree or disagree with the statement and then write notes to follow when making your speech. Make sure you have well-supported arguments.

Summary

Muslims believe that sex outside marriage is wrong because:

- the Qur'an only allows for sex between marriage partners
- children born outside marriage may have a less stable family life
- promiscuity makes a person vulnerable to sexually-transmitted diseases
- loving sexual relations unites a married couple
- adultery breaks up the family.

3.3 The purposes of a Muslim marriage and how these are shown in the wedding ceremony

Learning outcomes

By the end of this lesson you should be able to:

- outline the purposes of marriage in Islam
- identify the features of a Muslim wedding ceremony and explain how these show the purposes of marriage.

edexcel ⋮⋮⋮ key terms

Mahr – A sum of money placed in trust for a bride by her husband at the wedding.

Contract – The legal document of marriage.

Glossary

Nikah – The marriage contract.

Sacrament – Used by some people to mean a special agreement between God and man.

Walimah – Celebration of the marriage and a Sunnah of the Holy Prophet.

Family life is an extremely important part of Muslim society and marriage is the beginning of the family. It does not have to be a religious ceremony.

In Islam, marriages are not considered to be 'made in Heaven' between 'soulmates' destined for each other; they are not sacraments. They are social contracts that bring rights and obligations to both parties, and can only be successful when these are mutually respected and cherished.

Marriage in Islam is a **contract** signed between two people that establishes a commitment to each other and a willingness to take responsibility for each other. Both parties have clear duties laid down for them:

> 'The best of treasures is a good wife. She is pleasing in her husband's eyes... takes care of his possessions...' (Hadith)

> 'Men are protectors and maintainers of women because Allah has given the one more [strength] than the other and because they [men] support them [women] from their means.' (Surah 4)

It is not assumed that a couple will remain together forever regardless of circumstances. Islam is realistic, and aware that many marriages go wrong and break down for all sorts of reasons. However, most marriages start with the best of intentions, and the state of marriage is regarded as the ideal way for Muslims to live. There is a saying in Islam that whoever marries safeguards half his religion.

Celibacy (not having sexual relations) is disapproved of in Islam as it may lead to all sorts of psychological and physical tensions and problems. It is important, therefore, that persons getting married should do their utmost to make the partner happy and satisfied in every respect. Truly practising Muslims will keep to the rules, and may only have one sexual partner in the whole of their lives.

To follow the example of the Prophet Muhammad who married	To have children and bring them up as good Muslims
Why do Muslims marry?	
To have sex within the boundaries set by Allah	To share companionship and love

For discussion

1. Look at the four reasons given in the diagram in answer to 'Why do Muslims marry?' Which do you think would be the most important reason for you? Why?

2. Which do you think would be the most important reason for a Muslim? Why?

1 Stating in front of witnesses that you are free to marry. This is a legal requirement in Britain wherever you marry – in a church, a register office, or other licensed building.

3 Sermon and prayers by the imam. There does not have to be a religious person present but most Muslims like to hear readings from the Qur'an and prayers for the future of their marriage.

2 Signing the nikah and giving of **mahr**. The nikah is the contract that gives both husband and wife rights and responsibilities.

4 Walimah or wedding feast. The walimah is usually a meal and how long the celebrations last depends on the country where the wedding takes place.

Elements of a Muslim wedding

Activity

1 Compose an email to a friend describing a Muslim wedding ceremony. Explain in your email what was the most important part of the ceremony and explain why you thought this was important.

Create a chart that summarises what marriage is, the purpose of marriage and how this is represented in the Muslim marriage ceremony.

What marriage is	
The purpose of marriage	
Symbol in ceremony	

Summary

- Marriage is recommended in Islam.
- Muslims believe that marriage is important as it maintains family life.
- Marriage is a contract with rights and responsibilities for both parties.

3.4 Muslim attitudes to divorce

58

In Britain a divorce is given by the courts if it is judged that the marriage has 'irretrievably broken down'; this is usually granted because of adultery, unreasonable behaviour or desertion – when one partner leaves the other for a long time.

In the UK about a third of marriages end in divorce and there are about 160,000 divorces each year. People are more inclined to consider getting divorced than they were many years ago, for a number of reasons:

- it is no longer necessary to have both partners agree to the divorce
- women can now have financial stability without a husband
- divorced people are no longer considered to be wicked.

Reasons against divorce

- Muhammad hated divorce. *'The most detestable act that God has permitted is divorce.'* (Hadith)
- Marriage is the best state to be in because the Prophet married and did not divorce.
- Divorce is bad because it breaks up the family which is the most important institution in Islam. *'The best of you is the one who is best to his family.'* (Hadith)

Divorce in Islam

Divorce is allowed in Islam and there is clear guidance written in the Qur'an about how to divorce if there is no chance of the marriage surviving.

Most Muslims allow divorce as a last resort because it is a social contract and contracts can be broken. Relationships sometimes do not work out and it would be wrong to keep a couple together when they do not want to be.

'Either keep your wife honestly or put her away from you in kindness. Do not force a woman to stay with you who wishes to leave.' (Surah 2)

The Qur'an sets out procedures which have to be followed:

- the intention to divorce is announced
- there is a three-month waiting period when both parties have the chance to think about their marriage, seek help from family and friends and to try to reconcile the issue
- this waiting time also allows the wife to ascertain whether she is pregnant
- at the end of this time, if both parties agree, the divorce will become final and they are free to re-marry.

According to Islamic law only a husband has the right to divorce his wife. If a wife does not want to live with her husband she has a right to khul' – this means that she can ask her husband to divorce her and in return she may give up her dowry.

If the husband refuses to divorce her and she finds it impossible to live with him then she can go to a Muslim Qazi (judge) and file for the dissolution of their marriage.

A Muslim judge can dissolve Islamic marriage, but his first duty is always to save the marriage if possible.

Besides khul' a prospective wife can also make a condition in the marriage contract itself that would give her the right to a divorce later if necessary.

ResultsPlus
Build better answers

Explain why there are different Muslim attitudes to divorce. (8 marks)

 Basic, 1–2-mark answers

Students who get one or two marks will just give one developed reason. Lower-mark answers are likely to explain what the different attitudes are, without explaining why Muslims have these attitudes.

 Good, 3–6-mark answers

Answers that receive 3 or 4 marks will usually give two reasons, which are developed. Answers that receive 5 or 6 marks usually give three developed reasons. These answers will explain the different attitudes and why they are held.

▲ **Excellent, 7–8-mark answers**

The best answers will give four reasons, which are developed, although answers that only give one reason can still get full marks as long as the reason is explained in a lot of detail.

Activities

3 With a partner devise a questionnaire to find out what people think about divorce. Then ask at least ten people to complete your questionnaire. Ask both Muslims and non-Muslims. Compile the results with the rest of your class and then write a report stating your findings.

For discussion

Do you think that it is better to divorce than to remain in an unhappy marriage? Give two reasons for your answer.

Summary

- Divorce is allowed in Islam because marriage is a contract.
- The Qur'an gives clear guidance on matters of divorce.
- Divorce is not encouraged in Islam because Muhammad said it was the 'most hated thing' and because it breaks up the family unit.

3.5 Muslim teachings on family life

Learning outcomes

At the end of this lesson you should be able to:

- outline Muslim teachings on family life
- explain and evaluate the importance of the family in Muslim belief
- give your opinion on these beliefs and justify your opinion.

What is a family?

In the UK today there are many types of families. Traditionally a family consisted of a mother, a father and their children. If they lived as a small unit they were called a **nuclear family**. If they had grandparents or uncles and aunts living with them they were called an extended family. Extended families were the most common type of family in Britain before the Industrial Revolution.

In Britain today we also have a large number of single-parent families where one parent lives alone with their children as a result of divorce, separation, death or because the parent is unmarried. There are also **re-constituted families** and families with single-sex parents.

Muslims believe that parents and children living together as a family is the basis for a stable society and it is within the family that children learn about Allah and the Muslim faith.

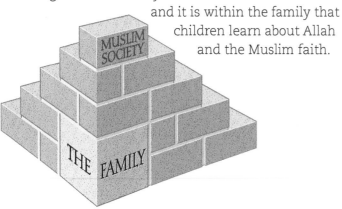

Activities

1 Some Muslims call the family the 'cornerstone of society'. Discuss with a friend what you think this means.

edexcel ::: key terms

Nuclear family – Mother, father and children living as a unit.

Re-constituted family – Where two sets of children (stepbrothers and stepsisters) become one family when their divorced parents marry each other.

Glossary

Extended family – Where parents, children and other relations (such as grandparents, aunts, uncles and cousins) all live together.

Single-parent family – One parent living alone with their children as a result of divorce, separation, death or because the parent is unmarried.

Same-sex family – Two same-sex parents and their children.

Why is the family so important?

The family provides the environment where children learn their values and the basic rules for good behaviour. Muslims believe that if the family is a strong unit then the rest of society will be secure. They believe that Allah gives children as a gift that should be cared for in order to make society a good and stable place in which to live.

There are many verses in the Qur'an and passages in the Hadith that set out how children should be brought up. These guidelines for parents and children are about caring for each other and showing respect for each other.

> 'He who has no compassion for our little ones and does not acknowledge the honour due to our elders is not one of us.' (Hadith)

Muhammad said that the extended family is very important and it is the duty of children to care for their parents when they get old.

> 'May his nose be rubbed in the dust who found his parents approaching old age and did not enter paradise serving them.' (Hadith)

I must provide for my family.

Teenagers need their own space to study.

Mum and Dad can't look after themselves any longer.

The house is so small we will be in each other's way.

For discussion

- In many societies elderly relatives are looked after in care homes. What are the advantages and disadvantages of this system?
- Are there more advantages than disadvantages of having an extended family (children, parents, grandparents) living together? Give reasons for your opinion.

Activities

2   Look at the table below, which shows some of the responsibilities of parents and children in Islam. The column for parents has been completed. With a partner discuss what you think might go into the children's column. Copy and complete the table.

Parents	Children
Bring their children up as good Muslims	
Keep a halal home	
Show love but don't be over-protective	
Give help and advice when necessary	
Don't force children to do more than they are able	
Give children a good education	
Treat children equally – no favourites	

ResultsPlus
Exam question report

Explain why family life is important in Islam. (8 marks) June 2007

How students answered

Many students received low marks for this question. This was mainly because they made the mistake of describing features of Muslim family life rather than explaining why it is important.

Most answers that received good marks for this question gave two developed reasons (4 marks) or three developed reasons (6 marks).

There were a few excellent answers to this question. Many of these linked the importance of the family to Islamic teachings.

Summary

- Muslims believe that family life is the basis for a good society.
- Parents have a duty to care for their children and bring them up as Muslims.
- Children must respect their parents and take care of them when they are old.
- Muhammad had a family and Muhammad is the example to follow.

3.6 How mosques help to keep the family together

62

Learning outcomes

By the end of this lesson you should be able to:

- describe and explain how mosques help with the upbringing of children
- describe and explain how mosques help keep the family together
- evaluate the role of the mosque in the upbringing of children, giving reasons for the different viewpoints
- evaluate the role of the mosque in keeping the family together.

Glossary

Mosque – Place for communal prayer and activities.

Special schools to teach the Qur'an

Special services at Eid

Activities at the mosque

Social centres with clubs for boys and girls

Help with financial difficulties

Friday Jumu'ah midday prayer for fathers and sons

Imams available to give advice in difficult situations

Activities

1 Look at the spider diagram and make a list of the things that happen at the mosque. Now link the ideas below with the events on your list.

- helps fathers and sons to spend time together
- teaches children about Islam
- gives advice about children's behaviour
- helps teenagers to be part of the Islamic community.

The mosque is very much the religious, social and educational centre of the Islamic community and is especially important in non-Muslim countries. A mosque is the focal point of a Muslim community. It is far more than just a place of worship – it is a resource centre, where groups of people come together for very different events.

A mosque is an education centre, a venue for luncheon clubs, a place where youth groups get together and where Muslim women can train for future employment.

Mosques are also important for youth education and all boys and girls aged from 5 to 15 attend classes in the evenings or at the weekend for religious instruction.

Adapted from Lancashire Mosques website

Muslim parents have a responsibility to bring their children up to be good Muslims. This begins at home with the mother teaching the children the basics of Islam and keeping a halal home. Also children learn from watching their parents. When they are old enough to begin going to the mosque their education is extended.

The mosque is more than a building; it is made up of a community of people who are striving to please Allah. One way of pleasing Allah is to help families who might be having difficulties. Here are some ways in which the mosque supports families:

giving zakat to help poor families

giving advice on legal matters such as divorce

after school clubs to teach children about Islam

social events that all the family can join in

a meeting place where parents can discuss any difficulties and celebrate successes with others

Activities

2 Visit your local mosque and make a list of all the activities that take place there. Highlight all those that you think would help with the upbringing of children.

3 Underneath your list answer the following question. How important do you think the role of the mosque is in helping with the upbringing of children? Give your reasons.

Activities

4 Prepare a leaflet for a mosque intended to help a Muslim family who have just moved to a new area. What activities might the mosque offer that would be useful to them? Why would these be important to help support the family unit? Give your reasons.

Summary

Mosques are at the centre of the Muslim community and help with family life by:

- helping to teach the children about Islam and how to live a life pleasing to Allah
- helping with financial difficulties when necessary
- organising family events to encourage the family to spend time together.

The mosque and family life

As we saw on pages 56–57, the family is very important in Islam. Anything that breaks the family unit is considered wrong, so the whole community work together to ensure that families are protected and happy.

3.7 Different methods of contraception and reasons for them

64

Lesson outcomes

By the end of this lesson you should be able to:

● explain why some people use contraception

● evaluate and give your opinion on these attitudes.

edexcel ::: key terms

Contraception – The deliberate prevention of pregnancy.

Since the Second World War in the UK **contraception** has become easily available and acceptable to the majority of people. Many people believe that there is no reason why anyone should become pregnant unless they want to.

Activities

1 (a) The newspaper headlines below were written to shock people. What did you feel when you read them? Were you shocked?

   (b) Do some research and find out how many teenage pregnancies have occurred in the past five years. Make a table showing your results.

Year	Number of pregnancies

TEENAGE PREGNANCIES ON THE INCREASE

▶ 'Sex education failing to halt teen pregnancy' (*Daily Telegraph, 30.12.07*)

▶ 'Nearly half of Norfolk teen pregnancies result in abortion' (*Norwich Evening News, 18.5.09*)

▶ 'Most teen pregnancies now end with an abortion' (*Daily Mail, 11.5.09*)

Contraception is the deliberate prevention of pregnancy by natural or artificial methods. It involves using one of a number of methods.

Artificial methods are:

- the pill – taken daily
- the morning after pill – taken within 72 hours of unprotected intercourse
- condoms
- contraceptive injection
- contraceptive implant
- the IUD (intrauterine device, also known as coil)
- sterilisation
- vasectomy.

Natural methods are:

- the rhythm method: planning sexual intercourse around the women's menstrual cycle to avoid the fertile time.

Why do people use contraception?

People who use contraception usually do so because they have decided that it is not appropriate for them to have children at this point in their lives. This may be because:

- some couples wish to plan when to have their family so that every child is a wanted child
- the couple or one partner doesn't want children
- they consider themselves too young or too old (for example, they may be teenagers at school unable to look after a baby or they may be a couple who have married later in life)
- they do not believe they would be good parents (for example, some people who have not had a happy childhood themselves might be worried about bringing up a child)

- they feel they could not provide financially or emotionally for a child (for example, they might be homeless, without jobs or already have a large family)
- they have a lifestyle that they feel would not be compatible with having a child (for example, they might have jobs that demand a lot of travelling or working unsocial hours)
- becoming pregnant would be harmful to the health of the mother.

One of the strongest arguments for the use of condoms is that they also help to protect against most sexually transmitted diseases. From one act of unprotected sex a person could contract HIV, which leads to AIDS.

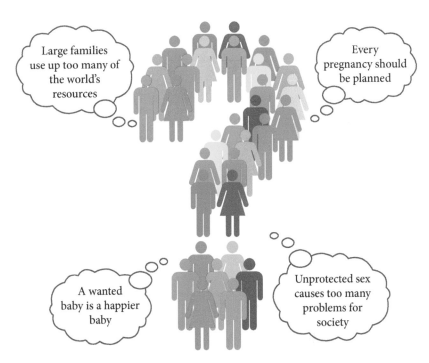

Activities

2   Look at the arguments above. With a friend discuss the statements and then prepare a speech for a debate on the arguments for and against the use of contraception.

Summary

- There are a number of different methods of contraception.
- The condom also helps protect against sexually transmitted diseases.

3.8 Muslim attitudes to contraception

Learning outcomes

By the end of this lesson you should be able to:

- outline Muslim teaching about contraception
- explain and evaluate Muslim attitudes towards contraception.

Islamic medicine has known about birth control for centuries. There are references to it in writings as early as the first century AD.

Islam teaches that life is a sacred gift from Allah:

> 'To Allah belongs the kingdom of the heavens and the earth. He creates what He pleases…' (Surah 42)

Children are also a gift:

> 'Allah bestows females upon whom He pleases and He bestows males upon whom He pleases; or He mixes them, males and females; and He makes whom He pleases barren.' (Surah 42)

1 Sexual activity can only take place within marriage.

2 The purpose of marriage and sex is to have children.

3 Islam is strongly pro-family and regards children as a gift from Allah.

4 The mother's health is important.

The Qur'an does not refer to contraception explicitly, but Muslims opposed to birth control often quote the Qur'an as saying '*You should not kill your children for fear of want*' (Surah 17:31, 6:151) and interpret this as including a ban on contraception as well as infanticide (killing children after birth).

In practice most Muslim authorities permit most methods of contraception to preserve the health of the mother or the well-being of the family.

Activities

1 List some of the ways that you think using contraception can help a family.

Why are some forms of contraception not acceptable to Muslims?

The way that the contraceptive stops pregnancy is a concern for some Muslims.

For most, a barrier method such as the cap or condom is acceptable, since the sperm and egg are prevented from meeting and so conception cannot take place. Many Muslims also accept the pill, as life is prevented from starting.

Contraceptive methods that do not prevent conception but cause a very early abortion are not accepted. So, for many Muslims, the coil and the morning after pill, which act after conception and prevent implantation, are considered by some to be the equivalent of an abortion and are therefore unacceptable.

Activities

2 Make a list of the contraceptive methods (use the list from the previous lesson) that would be acceptable to Muslims. Next to each one explain why this method is acceptable.

In a different colour, add to your list the methods that would not be acceptable to Muslims and explain why.

Using contraception with the aim of having a permanently child-free marriage is not accepted because one of the purposes of marriage is to have children. So sterilisation is not allowed because it prevents having children permanently.

ResultsPlus
Watch out!

In questions that ask for reasons for Muslim attitudes towards contraception some answers are weaker because they do not link religious teaching with the different Muslim attitudes.

For discussion

'A small family is a healthy family.' Do you agree? Give reasons for your answer and refer to Islam in your discussion.

Summary

- Some Muslims are against contraception because life is a gift from Allah.
- Most Muslims today accept some form of contraception as a responsible way of planning a family.
- Many Muslims agree with contraception to protect the health of the mother and the well-being of the family.
- Some Muslims only accept barrier methods of contraception because they believe that life begins at conception.

3.9 The media and marriage and family life

68

Love, marriage and divorce are popular topics with all forms of the media because they are part of everybody's life. Soap operas, films and newspaper headlines all record stories that reflect the joys and sorrows of relationships.

Here is an example taken from a newspaper:

EXCLUSIVE Guy Ritchie reveals why love in Madonna marriage died

MIRROR REVEALS FINAL THROES OF TROUBLED SUPERSTAR MARRIAGE

How Guy's happiness changed into misery

Activities

1 With a partner make a list of all the famous people that you have heard about who have got married or divorced recently. On your list put a cross besides any story that you think might have been exaggerated to try and make it more popular. What features of a report make it more interesting?

The character Masood Ahmed, played by Nitin Ganatra, is a postman in the soap opera EastEnders.

Some recent films that cover the issues of marriage and the family deal with the difficulties that can arise for Muslim teenagers in Britain.

In the comedy film *East is East*, a Pakistani father wants his children to marry within the faith of Islam but his own lifestyle does not set a good example for them.

In the film *Every Good Marriage Begins with Tears* the director explores the concerns of both traditional Muslim family members and some of the Anglicised children.

In *EastEnders* there have been two storylines involving the Muslim family, the Masoods, which raised a number of issues about family life. Zainab, the mother who is in her mid-forties, is devastated to find that she is pregnant. She says that she doesn't want the baby as she has already raised three children and wants to do something different with her life. This creates tension and arguments in the family as most Muslims believe that it would be wrong to have an abortion in these circumstances. The second controversial issue was raised by the revelations that Syed was involved in a homosexual relationship.

For discussion

1 Do you think soap operas such as *EastEnders* should have characters in them that represent Muslims? Give reasons for your answer.

2 How far do you think it is important for characters in films and on television to be realistic?

Activities

2 Imagine you are a television producer. Write an episode for a soap opera that might help non-Muslims understand the importance of the family for Muslims.

Summary

- Storylines about marriage and family life are very common in all forms of media as they are relevant for everyone. There are continuing debates about whether some of these stories are fair in their representation of religious families and people.

examzone

KnowZone
Marriage and the family

Quick quiz

1 What is **contraception**?

2 Name one barrier method of contraception.

3 What is **cohabitation**?

4 Define **adultery**.

5 List two attitudes of Muslims to divorce.

6 What is a **re-constituted family**?

7 What is a **nuclear family**?

8 Name one way that a mosque helps to keep families together.

9 What is **mahr**?

10 Name one of the purposes of marriage in Islam.

Plenary activity

Draw a spider diagram for each of the topics in this section. Put the name of the topic in the centre and then for the legs put in:

- any 'facts' or laws that you need to know

- arguments for and against each issue

- Muslim teachings on the issue

- different Muslim opinions

- your own opinion with reasons.

ResultsPlus
Top tip!

Candidates who give the best answers to questions on this topic remember that sex outside marriage covers both pre-marital and extra-marital sex. Deal with both in your answers.

Self-evaluation checklist

Read through the following list and evaluate how well you know and understand each of the topics.
How well have you understood the topics in this section? In the first column of the table below use the following code to rate your understanding:

Green – I understand this fully.

Orange – I am confident I can answer most questions on this.

Red – I need to do a lot more work on this topic.

In the second and third columns you need to think about:

● Whether you have an opinion on this topic and could give reasons for that opinion, if asked.

● Whether you can give the opinion of someone who disagrees with you and give reasons for this alternative opinion.

Content covered	My understanding is red/orange/green	Can I give my opinion?	Can I give an alternative opinion?
● Changes in attitudes in the UK to marriage, divorce, family life, sex outside marriage, and homosexuality.			
● Muslim attitudes to sex outside marriage.			
● The purpose of marriage in Islam and how this is shown through the wedding ceremony.			
● Attitudes of Muslims to homosexuality.			
● Muslim teachings on the importance of family life.			
● How mosques help with the upbringing of children and explain how this helps keep the family together.			

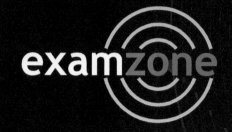

KnowZone
Marriage and the family

Introduction

In the exam you will see a choice of two questions on this section. Each question will include four tasks, which test your knowledge, understanding and evaluation of the material covered. A 2-mark question will ask you to define a term; a 4-mark question will ask your opinion on a point of view; an 8-mark question will ask you to explain a particular belief or idea; a 6-mark question will ask for your opinion on a point of view and ask you to consider an alternative point of view.

Choose the question you can answer best – remembering you need to answer all parts of the question you choose!

You must give your opinion, but make sure you do give two clear and properly thought-out reasons. These can be ones you have learned in class, even if they are not your own opinion. You mustn't use terms such as 'rubbish' or 'stupid' as these don't show that you are able to think things through carefully.

In your answer you should state whether or not you agree with the statement. You should also give reasons for your opinion.

In either (i) or (ii) you must refer to Islam.

Mini exam paper

(a) What is **cohabitation**? (2 marks)

(b) Do you think divorce is better than an unhappy marriage? Give **two** reasons for your point of view. (4 marks)

(c) Explain why family life is important for Muslims. (8 marks)

(d) 'No Muslim should be homosexual.'

In your answer you should refer to Islam.

(i) Do you agree? Give reasons for your opinion. (3 marks)

(ii) Give reasons why some people may disagree with you. (3 marks)

Here you need to give a short, accurate definition. You do not need to write more than one clear sentence.

The word 'explain' means you should give details of activities religious families may carry out together or ways in which they share their faith, but you must also show how these may lead to belief in Allah. This question is worth 8 marks so you must be prepared to spend some time answering it. You will also be assessed on your use of language in this question.

Now you have to give the opposite point of view, again using material you have learned during your studies. You don't have to say what you think about these alternative points of view, but you do need to show you understand why they are just as important to consider as your own opinion.

Mark scheme

(a) You can earn **2 marks** for a correct answer, and **1 mark** for a partially correct answer.

(b) To earn up to the full **4 marks** you need to give two reasons and develop them. Two brief reasons or only one developed reason will earn **2 marks**.

(c) You can earn **7–8 marks** by giving up to four reasons, but the fewer reasons you give, the more you must develop them. Because you are being assessed on use of language, you also need to take care to express your understanding in a clear style of English, and make some use of specialist vocabulary.

(d) To go beyond **3 marks** for the whole of this question you must refer to at least one religion. The more you are able to develop your reasons the more marks you will earn. Three simple reasons can earn you the same mark as one fully developed reason.

ResultsPlus
Build Better Answers

(d) 'No Muslim should be homosexual.'
In your answer you should refer to Islam.
(i) Do you agree? Give reasons for your opinion. (3 marks)
(ii) Give reasons why some people may disagree with you. (3 marks)

Student answer	Comments	Improved student answer
I agree with the statement that no Muslim should be homosexual. I think this because homosexuals cannot get married and have children, which is one of the teachings of Islam. Also homosexually is forbidden by the Qur'an.	This is a good answer to part (i) of the question as the candidate clearly gives their opinion with two reasons to support it. However the candidate does not attempt the second part of the question at all and therefore could significantly improve their answer.	I agree with the statement that no Muslim should be homosexual. I think this because homosexuals cannot get married and have children, which is one of the teachings of Islam. Also homosexually it forbidden by the Qur'an. A few Muslims would disagree with my view. They would think that as Allah has created everyone as they are, he has created some people as homosexual and therefore it is part of his plan so it cannot be wrong.

Religion and community cohesion

Introduction

In this section you will consider issues that arise from humans being unique and different from any other creatures. You will learn what Muslims believe about how people should be treated and their attitudes towards gender roles, racism, prejudice and discrimination. You will consider the advantages of living in a multi-faith society and you will learn how the teaching of the Qur'an and Hadith promote racial harmony and community cohesion and inspire Muslims to work towards a peaceful and happy society. You will reflect on your own understanding of how to create equality and peace in the world.

Learning outcomes for this section

By the end of this section you should be able to:

- give definitions and examples of the key terms
- outline changing attitudes towards gender roles in the UK
- explain and evaluate Muslim attitudes towards equal rights for women in religion
- understand how the UK works as a multi-ethnic society, and how the government works to promote community cohesion
- express your opinion on issues of racism and discrimination in the UK today
- outline the work of a Muslim organisation to help asylum seekers
- explain why Muslims should promote racial harmony
- outline and explain Muslim attitudes to other religions
- express your view on the advantages and disadvantages of the UK as a multi-faith society today
- describe ways in which religions work to promote community cohesion
- evaluate the presentation of religion and community cohesion in the media.

edexcel ⠿ key terms

community cohesion	interfaith marriage	prejudice	religious freedom
discrimination	multi-ethnic society	racial harmony	religious pluralism
ethnic minority	multi-faith society	racism	sexism

Fascinating fact

In 2008 in UK primary schools, 21.9 per cent of students were ethnic-minority pupils, while in secondary schools the figure was 17.7 per cent.

In some parts of London, children from ethnic-minority families account for more than nine in ten school places.

(Source: RAISEonline)

Human beings are a species of mammal. They are different shapes, sizes and colours, but all human beings.

1 (a) Can you think of any other mammals where the species is multi-coloured, multi-sized, etc.? Make a list.

(b) Why is it that we do not discriminate between these species but some people do with human beings?

2 Why did this discrimination start? Can you identify any areas where there is still discrimination? Have you experienced discrimination? Discuss with a partner how you think it might feel to be treated differently because of your colour, race, sex or age.

3 Look at the information given in the Fascinating fact box. Do you think schools will need to change the way they manage the curriculum?

4.1 Changing attitudes to the roles of men and women in the UK

Learning outcomes

By the end of this lesson you should be able to:

- outline and explain the changing roles of men and women in the UK
- express your own opinions about gender roles
- explain the inequalities that remain and give your opinion on how things might be improved still further.

Glossary

Gender – Being male or female.

Equality – The state of everyone having equal rights regardless of their gender, race or class.

You start by sinking into his arms and end up with your arms in his sink!

Activities

1 What do you think this piece of graffiti is saying about the rights of women? Is it fair today? Was it fair 50 years ago?

What changes have there been in attitudes to the role of women in the last 50 years?

A century ago only 15 per cent of married women worked outside the home. Having been given equal voting rights in 1928, and working in traditionally male jobs during the Second World War as replacements for the men who had gone to fight, many women expected to continue to work alongside men and not just stay at home as housekeepers.

However, with many soldiers returning from the war and in need of work it was expected that women would return to menial jobs. Women's organisations campaigned for equal rights. Some jobs were considered very 'unfeminine' e.g. doctors, mill owners, factory managers. Even in the 21st century there are comparatively few women engineers. Some advances towards equality have been made, but there is sill some way to go before men and women are fully equal.

In 1970 an act was passed giving women equal pay with men when doing equal work.

In 1979 Margaret Thatcher became Britain's first female prime minister and became a role model for many women as someone who could have a home, children and an important job. However, even now many commentators speak of her success as being due to her 'masculine' traits.

Men should earn more as they have families to support

Women aren't as productive as men as they have lots of time off to have babies

Women are too emotional to be good leaders

Many women are single parents and have children to support so they won't focus on their work

Men are physically stronger so are better at being engineers and builders

Men think more logically then women so are better in management roles

Women are better in the caring professions

Although there is now equal pay for equal work many women are in low-paid jobs because they work part-time in order to look after their children or because they have taken time off work to raise their children.

As we've seen, a century ago only 15 per cent of married women worked outside the home. However, after the two world wars attitudes changed, because during the wars women had to do the work of men who had gone to fight, and after the war ended, women's organisations campaigned for equal rights.

For discussion

1 How far do you think the pictures above reflect the changing roles of men and women?

2 Do you think more needs to be done to break the stereotype of 'superman'/'little woman'? Give reasons for your answer.

Activities

2 Read the statements in the circles above. Choose two of the statements and write a paragraph explaining whether you agree or disagree. Give at least two reasons for your point of view.

Summary

- Since 1970, women legally have equal rights in the workplace.
- Men are now taking on some of the more traditional women's roles – nursing, childminding, etc.
- Many cartoons and comedians still stereotype the roles of men and women.

4.2 Muslim attitudes to equal rights for women in religion

Learning outcomes

By the end of this lesson you should be able to:

● describe and explain Muslim teachings on the role and status of women in religion

● express your own opinions on different Muslim attitudes towards women in religion.

> *'Allah created men and women from a single soul.'*
> (Surah 4.1)

There is no **sexism** in the Qur'an; it is clearly stated that men and women are equal in the sight of God because Allah made man and woman from a single soul. Islam teaches that the only thing that distinguishes people in the sight of God is their obedience to Allah and their level of God-consciousness.

> *'Whoever works righteousness, man or woman, and has faith, verily to him we will give a new life.'* (Surah 16)

Islamic law guarantees certain rights to women:

● she can own property

● she can have a job

● she should be paid equal pay for equal work

● she has the right to inherit property

● she has control of her wealth

● she has the right to get a divorce

● she has the right to education

edexcel key terms

Sexism – Discriminating against people because of their gender (being male or female).

Glossary

Unbiased – A fair approach to an issue; not affected by prejudice.

However Islam teaches that men and women have equal but specific, different roles to play in life.

> *'All people are equal… as the teeth of a comb… nor a male over a female'.* (Hadith)

> *'Men are the protectors and maintainers of women because Allah has given them more strength.'* (Surah 42)

Activity

1 Often newspapers and television reports highlight the role of Muslim women in different countries. Do some research and find one report. (You will find some on the Internet.) Comment on the report. Do you think the report was unbiased? How far did the report focus on the culture and traditions of the country and how far did it focus on Islam? Give reasons for your point of view.

Most Muslims believe that the role of the woman as a mother is more important than any other role because family values are established in the home. If family values are good then society will be better.

Muhammad said 'paradise lies at the feet of your mother'. This encourages Muslim women to take pride in their role as homemakers. Even those Muslim women who seek greater equality with men do so within the context of wanting choice rather than the desire to abandon their role as a homemaker.

What does equal but different mean in practice?

	Both	Men	Women
Religious practice	Follow the Five Pillars Equal Judgement at the last day based on their faith and obedience to Allah	Friday prayers at the mosque are compulsory	Attendance at the mosque is voluntary – depending on her family commitments
Daily responsibility	Own property and run a business	Responsible for the financial welfare of the family	Duty to bear children and bring them up as Muslims Keep a halal home Choose to work outside the home
Daily life and relationships	Right to a good education Become teachers, doctors, lawyers etc.	Physically stronger Protectors of women	Emotionally weaker Can expect to be cared for

Attitudes to women in Islamic society

Traditional	Modern
Equal but different roles	Equal in religion and education
Bring up children and keep halal home	Women can have jobs but priority is to bring up children
No need to go to mosque	Worship in mosque but separately
Men and women should always be separate	Women can be teachers as Aisha was – she helped many males with interpretations of the Hadith, and she also led the army in battle
Physiologically not suited to leadership	
'And they (women) have rights similar to those (of men) over them, and men are a degree above them.' (Surah 2)	*'Believing men and women… humble themselves, fast… give charity… God has prepared forgiveness and a great reward.'* (Surah 33)
'Men are protectors of women.' (Surah 4)	*'Men and women are equal in the eyes of God, and that we are like a garment for each other to protect one another.'* (Surah 2)
'And when you ask (his wives) for anything you want, ask them from behind a screen, that is purer for your hearts and for their hearts.' (Surah 5)	*'Never will I suffer to be lost the work of any of you, male or female.'* (Surah 3)

For discussion

Recent research shows that more women than men are converting to Islam. Muslim women are also *choosing* to wear the veil. Why do you think this is?

Activities

2   More women are converting to Islam than men. The most common reason given is that Islam gives them security and protection. Imagine that you are interviewing a recent female convert. Choose some questions you might ask her and then with a partner role-play the interview and record her answers. At the end give your point of view about the role of women in Islam.

Summary

There are two main attitudes to the role of women in Muslim society:

- those who believe that because of biological differences women should remain at home because of the teaching of the Qur'an
- those who believe that men and women should be equal in all things also based on the teaching of the Qur'an but also on historical evidence from the time of the Prophet.

4.3 The United Kingdom as a multi-ethnic society

Learning outcomes

By the end of the lesson you should be able to:

- define what is meant by a multi-ethnic society
- describe the problem of racism
- explain how the UK became a multi-ethnic society
- explain some of the advantages of living in a multi-ethnic society
- give your opinion, with reasons, about these issues.

edexcel ⠿ key terms

Ethnic minority – A member of an ethnic group (race) that is much smaller than the majority group.

Multi-ethnic society – Many different races and cultures living together in one society.

Racism – The belief that some races are superior to others.

However, in the same time period, only 198,000 British citizens emigrated abroad, mostly going to live in southern Europe, Australia and New Zealand.

A multi-ethnic society

The UK is a **multi-ethnic** country, which means that it is made up of many different races, cultures and nationalities living together as one society.

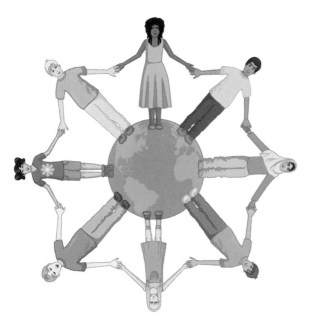

Recently, there has been large-scale immigration into the UK from the countries of Eastern Europe, particularly Poland. This is largely because these countries recently joined the European Union, which gave their citizens the right to work in other European Union countries. Between 2004 and 2006, for example, there were more than 600,000 Eastern Europeans who came to live and work in the UK. Many work either in building or the retail business.

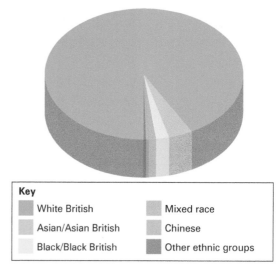

Key

■ White British	■ Mixed race
■ Asian/Asian British	■ Chinese
■ Black/Black British	■ Other ethnic groups

The ethnic make-up of the total population of the UK.

Activities

1. Look at the chart above, and then answer the following questions:

   (a) Which is the largest ethnic group in the UK?

   (b) What is the largest non-white group? Why do you think this is?

   (c) Which groups do you think would be called **ethnic minorities**?

   (d) Do you think it's right that citizens of the European Union should be able to work freely in other countries? What are the advantages and disadvantages?

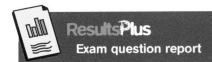

ResultsPlus
Exam question report

What is a **multi-ethnic society**? (2 marks) June 2007

How students answered

Most of the candidates who received 0 marks for this question got confused and defined 'multi-faith' instead of 'multi-ethnic' society.

There were only a few answers that received 1 mark for being partly correct. Most of these answered that a multi-ethnic society is a mixture of different people.

Most candidates wrote excellent answers that explained a multi-ethnic society is one made up of different races and different cultures.

Are there problems?

Over the past 50 years, as more people come into Britain from different countries, there have been many incidents of **racism**, where people are treated badly because of their race. Much has been done to educate people against racism and anti-discrimination laws have been passed by government. However, even in areas like sport there are still incidences of name calling and racist jokes.

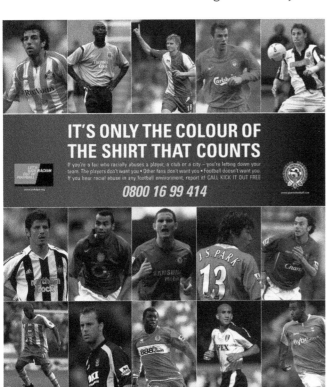

Activities

2 Write a poem or a rap against racism. Perform it to your class.

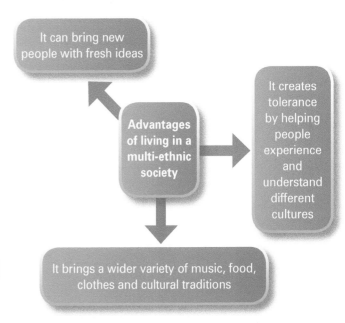

It can bring new people with fresh ideas

Advantages of living in a multi-ethnic society

It creates tolerance by helping people experience and understand different cultures

It brings a wider variety of music, food, clothes and cultural traditions

For discussion

Do you think there are more advantages or disadvantages to living in a multi-ethnic society? Give reasons for your answer, with examples.

Summary

- The UK is a multi-ethnic society.
- This used to cause problems of racism, which still linger today, though the situation has improved.
- Being a multi-ethnic society has many advantages, especially those concerned with understanding and appreciating different cultures and beliefs.

A poster from the campaign 'Let's kick racism out of football', established in 1993.

4.4 Government action to promote community cohesion

82

Learning outcomes

By the end of this lesson you should be able to:

- outline and explain what is meant by community cohesion
- describe some government measures to encourage community cohesion
- evaluate the role of government in promoting community cohesion.

edexcel ::: key terms

Community cohesion – A common vision and shared sense of belonging for all groups in society.

Discrimination – Treating people less favourably because of their ethnicity/gender/colour/sexuality/age/class.

Prejudice – Believing some people are inferior or superior without even knowing them.

Activities

1 First impressions. If you met these girls for the first time dressed like this what differences would you identify?

'Community cohesion is what must happen in all communities to enable different groups of people to get on well together.

A key contributor to community cohesion is integration, which is what must happen to enable new residents and existing residents to adjust to one another.'

(A statement about community cohesion from the government report of February 2008)

Community cohesion means different communities living together and sharing four things in common:

- A common vision and sense of belonging
- Making strong and positive relationships with people of different races
- Appreciating and valuing the differences
- Ensuring equal opportunities for all in the community

Community cohesion

What is the government doing?

In order to foster community cohesion in the UK, in 2009 the government promised that each area received the following.

- Money to help integrate new arrivals to an area – this could be used for housing, language lessons, information packs giving help to new migrants and setting out their rights and responsibilities.

- Money to establish good youth projects that encourage different social and ethnic groups to mix and work together. This should foster greater understanding of each other.

- Help in setting up groups to encourage good citizenship, which is about how we behave to one another and how we develop the skills to cope with a rapidly changing world and continue to trust one another.

- Help to set up specialist integration teams and cohesion teams that will work to support local councils in managing any major changes in the local population, e.g. provision and support for people to be able to translate documents and learn English (not being able to speak English is one of the biggest barriers to integration).

Many laws have been passed to prevent **prejudice** and **discrimination**. Community cohesion is about setting up positive ways to enable people from different ethnic, religious and social backgrounds to work together to strengthen the local community.

Activities

2 Search your local authority website to find out what things they have put in place to promote community cohesion.

Schools and community cohesion

Schools have a responsibility to help children and young people to learn to understand others, to value diversity whilst also promoting shared values. They should support awareness of human rights and how to apply and defend these rights.

Schools are encouraged to set up links with other schools in their area as well as internationally so that students have access to a wide variety of cultures.

Activities

3 What does it mean to 'value diversity'? Give examples.

4 Do you think your school does enough to encourage students to learn about other cultures and social groups? Make a list of activities that you think would help community cohesion in your school community.

For discussion

'It is better to help people mix than just make laws against racism.' Give reasons for your point of view.

Summary

- Community cohesion is a positive way of getting people together to share resources and ideas in both the local and the worldwide community.

- It is intended to help build strong relationships and a feeling of belonging across all social, ethnic and age groups.

4.5 The work of one Muslim organisation to help asylum seekers in the UK

Learning outcomes

By the end of this lesson you should be able to:

- outline the work of one Muslim organisation in the UK that helps asylum seekers
- explain why the organisation does this work
- evaluate the importance of the work.

Glossary

Asylum seeker – Someone who looks for protection and shelter in another country.

Sadaqah – Voluntary charitable giving.

Zakah – Charitable tax given by all Muslims once a year.

How do people become asylum seekers?

Activities

1 Break into groups of seven. Each member of the group should take on the role of a family member from the list below. Read the background information and then role-play the discussion the family have about the possibility of seeking asylum.

What do you and your group decide to do and why?

Members of the family

DAD: Journalist on a local paper

MUM: Has just had a baby

GRANNY: Is in a wheelchair and cannot leave the house

UNCLE ALI: Very active in the local mosque and has been in prison for his political beliefs; he can only walk slowly

CHILDREN: There are three other children of school age.

Background

Two months ago
Generals from the army took over the country. There was gunfire everywhere and tanks on the streets. Many people were killed, others were arrested. The military leaders imposed a curfew, so people were not allowed out at night.

One month ago
Dad found out that a lot of people who were trade union leaders had been arrested or had gone missing.

Two weeks ago
A local newspaper that supports the army published a list of people in the town that it said were enemies of the state. On the list were Dad's and Ali's names.

Last week
Mum heard that in the next town the army had arrested some women because they were looking for their husbands. Some children from the town had been taken hostage.

Two days ago
A friend rang up Uncle Ali and told him to get out of the town as he had heard that some people were planning to kill him and burn the house down.

Yesterday
Friends at school told the children that snatch squads of soldiers were searching people and arrested some members of Dad's trade union.

Today
The family heard gunfire in the town and trucks full of soldiers are arriving. There are roadblocks checking cars and all trains are searched.

The family [your group] meet to discuss the situation – what should they do? You could leave and seek asylum overseas. It is one hour by car to the border, or a week's journey on foot.

What happens when asylum seekers arrive in Britain?

On arrival in Britain asylum seekers should immediately declare their intention – that is that they wish to stay here for safety. They can stay with relatives or friends or some will be accommodated in hostels close to the airport. If they have already been granted refugee status by the UN and are part of a resettlement programme they will be able to move to the area where they will settle to live after about three days.

What help do they need?

If the asylum seekers have no family or friends they may need help to find food, clothing, accommodation and legal advice.

How do Muslims help?

There are many Muslim organisations in Britain that work to help asylum seekers. In 2008 the Scottish Islamic Association organised a 'Qurbani' distribution. This was using money raised at the end of Eid to provide food and clothing for refugees in Glasgow. Another organisation, The Centre for the Muslim Community in Southwark, gives help to refugees and asylum seekers, particularly women. Their help includes the following things:

- advice
- support
- counselling
- health/recreational activities for women
- youth activities
- lunch club for older people
- adult education project for newly arrived asylum seekers/refugees
- English classes, computer studies
- crèche facilities
- supplementary school.

Muslims and charity

Giving to charity is an integral part of the Islamic faith. The third obligatory pillar of Islam is zakah, where a person must give away a percentage of their income to help others. It comprises 2.5 per cent of surplus earnings at the end of the year. Muslims are also encouraged to make extra voluntary payments – sadaqah – to the needy.

The teaching of the Qur'an is:

> 'True righteousness... belief in Allah, the last day, and the angels, and the book and the prophets; and to spend of your wealth... for kinsfolk, for orphans and the needy and the wayfarer... to be steadfast in prayer and practise regular charity.' (Surah 2)

> 'How can you call yourself a believer while your brother goes hungry'. (Hadith)

Muslims believe that it is pleasing to Allah to help others and it is also their duty.

Activities

2 Look at the list above and make another list showing how these activities would be useful for people who have just arrived in Britain. Find out if there is a similar organisation in your area.

Summary

- Asylum seekers come to Britain to escape danger and persecution in their own country.
- Muslims help asylum seekers because it is part of their religious duty.

4.6 Why Muslims should promote racial harmony

Learning outcomes

By the end of this lesson you should be able to:

● outline and explain the teaching of Islam on racial harmony

● evaluate the role of Muslims in promoting racial harmony.

edexcel key terms

Racial harmony – Different races/colours living together happily.

Islamic teaching on racial harmony

● All humans were created by Allah therefore all are equal.

● Muhammad said that no race is superior to another in his last sermon.

● Muhammad set an example of equality by having an African as his first prayer caller.

● Muhammad emphasised the belief in the ummah – the world-wide community of Muslims.

'All people are equal... as the teeth of a comb. No Arab can claim merit over a non-Arab, nor a white over a black person, nor a male over a female.' (Hadith)

In the UK Muslims make up 3.3 per cent of the population. There are about 1.6 billion Muslims in the world. This number is spread all over the world so that all races and colours are part of the Muslim community – the ummah. This is seen very clearly on hajj when over two million Muslims from around the world gather to pray to Allah.

Activities

1 Look at the pictures. Write down your first impression of the images. What do you see that clearly shows equality amongst this huge number of people? Can you think of two other things that happen on hajj that show racial equality?

Allah and living in racial harmony

Muslims believe in tawhid – the oneness of Allah. This is the idea that Allah, as the only god, created the world to be a harmonious whole with everything working together for the glory of Allah. All human beings are called equally to submit to Allah in order to have happiness on Earth and reward in the life after death.

Belief in tawhid is shown in a number of ways.

1 Accepting the main beliefs

(i) Tawhid – this belief affects every part of a Muslim's life and determines what decisions are made.

(ii) Qur'an – the belief that this book is the final revealed word of Allah ensures that all Muslims have clear guidance in their lives.

(iii) Risalah – the belief that the teaching and example of the Prophet guides all Muslims.

(iv) Akhirah – the promise of reward or punishment after death helps Muslims focus on the will of Allah.

2 The Five Pillars

(i) Everyone praying five times a day at set times, saying the same words, facing the same direction and in the mosque standing shoulder to shoulder regardless of wealth, rank or colour.

(ii) Muslims worldwide observing Ramadan.

(iii) Giving zakah to help everyone, regardless of race.

(iv) Muslims worldwide going on hajj.

(v) Muslims have to declare their faith in Allah and the Prophet.

For discussion

How far do you think sharing the same beliefs and practices stops racism?

So Muslims all over the world, regardless of race or colour, are united in their worship of and obedience to Allah. Common beliefs and common values mean that there is no room for racism as all Muslims are members of Allah's community – the ummah.

Muhammad said: '*None of you will have faith until he wishes for his brother or sister what he would like for himself.*' (Hadith)

Malcolm X

Malcolm X has been described as one of the greatest and most influential African Americans in history. He is credited with raising the self-esteem of black Americans and reconnecting them with their African heritage. He contributed to the spread of Islam in the black community in the United States. His early teaching changed when he separated from the group called the Nation of Islam, which he believed had become corrupt. After going on hajj, Malcolm X expressed a view of white people and racism that represented a deep change from the philosophy he had held as a minister of the Nation of Islam. In a famous letter from Makkah he wrote that the white people he had met during his pilgrimage had forced him to 'rearrange' his thinking about race and 'toss aside some of his previous conclusions'.

He began to teach that both black and white should work together to combat racism; this led to his assassination in 1965.

Activities

2 Malcolm X said that going on hajj changed his ideas about racism. What do you think he meant? Give reasons for your opinion.

Summary

- Muslims believe that as Allah made every human being, human beings are all equal regardless of race or colour.
- Everyone has the right to be treated equally and Muslims have a duty to treat people equally.

4.7 Differences in Muslim attitudes to other religions

Learning outcomes

By the end of this lesson you should be able to:

- outline and explain the different Muslim attitudes towards other religions
- evaluate the idea that one religion can have the whole truth.

edexcel ::: key terms

Religious freedom – The right to practise your religion and to change your religion.

Religious pluralism – Accepting all religions as having an equal right to exist.

What do Muslims believe?

All Muslims believe in **religious freedom**. In the Qur'an it says 'there is no compulsion in religion'. This does not mean that all religions are equal because Muslims believe that only the Qur'an contains the full and final truth. It means that all religions should have the freedom to practise providing they do not harm Islam.

Glossary

People of the Book – The name for Jews and Christians in the Qur'an.

Super highway.

Meandering path.

Some Muslims believe in religious pluralism and accept that all religions have an equal right to exist. A few Muslims think that all religions are different paths to the same God because the Qur'an says there should be no compulsion in religion.

For discussion

In his book *Understanding Islam*, C.T. Hewer describes Muslims as seeing Islam as the superhighway of God's guidance while other religions are meandering paths.

What do you think he means?

Muslims believe that Allah revealed the final message to Muhammad: 'this day I have perfected your religion' (Surah 5) and that all other holy men, e.g. Abraham and Jesus, only had part of the truth. So their followers need to convert to Islam as the one true faith if they wish to go to Paradise.

Muslims will live with and tolerate Jews and Christians, called 'People of the Book' in the Qur'an, because they have part of the truth but they must not be a threat to them or to the religion of Islam.

Activity

Belief	Islam	Christianity	Judaism
Muhammad as a prophet			
One god	yes	yes	yes
Jesus as a prophet			
Jesus as son of God			
Abraham as a prophet			
Heaven			
al'Jannah			

1 Copy, complete and then extend the above table. Find out as much as you can about the differences and similarities between these three religions.

However, Muslims believe that followers of religions that are considered polytheistic (having more than one god) are guilty of shirk (making something equal with Allah). They will be excluded from Paradise.

Any religion claiming to have received a revelation from Allah after the Qur'an was given to Muhammad is also considered to be wrong.

ResultsPlus
Exam question report

Explain why there are different Muslim attitudes to other religions. (8 marks) June 2007

How students answered

Over half the candidates scored poorly on this question. Most of these described the different attitudes rather than explaining why there are different attitudes and therefore could not gain more than 2 marks.

Good answers gave several reasons why there are different attitudes, though many did not explain the reasons.

There were some excellent answers, which gave four developed reasons. Many of these answers linked the reasons to teachings in the Qur'an.

Summary

- Some Muslims believe that only Islam has Allah's true message and that the Qur'an teaches that only Muslims will go to Paradise.
- Other Muslims believe that Jews and Christians will go to Paradise as the Qur'an says in Surah 5 that the People of the Book who *'believe in God and the Last Day, and work righteousness, on them shall be no fear.'*
- A few Muslims believe that other religions are paths to Allah because the Qur'an talks about other prophets being sent to different people at different times.

4.8 The UK as a multi-faith society

Learning outcomes

By the end of this lesson you should be able to:

- outline and explain what a multi-faith society is
- evaluate the advantages and disadvantages of living in a multi-faith society.

edexcel ::: key terms

Multi-faith society – Many different religions living together in one society.

Is Britain a multi-faith society?

In some countries almost everyone belongs to the same religion. Today there are members of every religion living in Britain. Some groups are very small and some are very large. All are given freedom to practise their religion without fear of persecution. In some areas of the country, where one religion might be stronger than another, school holidays are adjusted so that the worshippers can celebrate their festivals more easily. Britain allows freedom of worship to all religions and has laws that punish anyone who tries to stop this freedom. So Britain is a **multi-faith society**.

Why is it good to live in a multi-faith society?

- You can learn about a variety of beliefs.
- You can understand more about these beliefs and decide which one you think is best.
- It can help you to be sure of your own belief.
- It creates tolerance amongst different faith groups.
- It helps people to live together in harmony.

The cartoon on the opposite page demonstrate some things that people say about living in a multi-faith society.

Activities

1 Look at the symbols and identify which religions they represent. Can you name the building where the followers of each religion would worship? Do you know which of these religions is practised in your area? List some of the things you would look for.

For discussion

'It is easier to live in a society where there is only one religion.' Give reasons for your point of view.

I like reading the different religious stories

I like to learn about different weddings

It makes me understand my own religion better

Finding out new things is exciting

I like the different festivals

All these people enjoy learning about different religious activities as it helps them understand their friends and stops misunderstandings. Sometimes finding out about another person's beliefs can make your own beliefs stronger.

Fascinating fact

In recent years the government has passed laws to protect religious freedom. These laws include the:

- Employment Equality (Religion or Belief) Regulations 2003
- Racial and Religious Hatred Act 2006
- Equality Act 2006 (part 2, 2007)
- Human Rights Act 1998.

Activities

2 Think about the comments in the speech bubbles. Can you think of any more advantages? Now consider if there are any problems caused by a multi-faith society. Make a collage with the good things on one side and any problems you can think of on the other.

ResultsPlus
Watch out!

Remember: multi-faith is about different religions, multi-ethnic is about different cultures. You must not mix them up!

Summary

- There are many different faiths in the UK. All people are free to follow whatever religion they wish.
- The advantages of a multi-faith society are that people can learn about other religions and this creates tolerance.
- The disadvantages are that some people might cause friction because they believe their religion is the right one.

4.9 Issues raised by multi-faith societies

Learning outcomes

By the end of this lesson you should be able to:

● outline and explain the issues that religions can face in a multi-faith society

● evaluate the extent of these issues giving your own point of view with reasons.

edexcel ▦ key terms

Interfaith marriage – Marriage where the husband and wife are from different religions.

What are the issues?

As more religious people mix with those of different faiths or no faith there are a number of things that could cause them concern:

Supposing I fall in love with someone from a different religion?

Will other religious people want to convert me to their faith?

What will my children learn about? Will they want to stay in my religion?

Will the mix of religions cause confusion so that no one really understands any of them?

Interfaith marriage

Some religions have very clear guidance on what should happen if someone from their faith wishes to marry outside their religion.

In Islam there is a saying that 'marriage is half your religion' and Muhammad said that the most important thing in choosing a marriage partner was that they were a pious follower of Islam. Muslim males are allowed to marry Jewish or Christian women but Muslim women may not do the same, as in Islam the child takes on the religion of the father. If men wish to marry someone from any other religion then the non-Muslim female partner must convert to Islam.

Activities

1 Imagine you have received a letter that asks for your help in solving one of the above issues. With a partner write your reply. It might be that there is not a straightforward answer so be prepared to give all the points of view that you think might help the writer of the letter sort out their ideas.

For discussion

Read the speech bubbles of the young people opposite. What would you advise each of them to do? How do you think these difficulties might be overcome?

My friends are trying to get me to go church with them but as a Muslim I would rather not.

My grandparents tell me different things – who do I believe?

If I marry someone from a different religion my parents might not speak to me again.

Conversion

Many religions believe that their followers will be the only ones to go to Heaven and so they set out to win others to their belief – they try to convert them. This can cause offence as it sounds as though they are saying their religion is better than anyone else's. It can also seem as though they are going against the principles of religious freedom.

Conflict can be caused because some people might feel inferior if others try to convert them.

Activities

2 Find out what Muslims believe about converting people to Islam. Write a short answer to the question: 'No one has the right to force a religion on you.' Do you agree? Give reasons for your answer and show that you have thought about another point of view.

3 In some parts of Britain the councils are so afraid of offending different religions that they have decided either to celebrate every religious festival or none at all. Do you think this is right in a multi-faith country?

ResultsPlus
Build better answers

Explain why trying to convert people may cause problems in a multi-faith society. (8 marks)

■ **Basic, 1–2-mark answers**
Basic answers only focus on one reason, or they offer a variety of reasons without explaining them.

● **Good, 3–6-mark answers**
These answers offer one developed reason (or two reasons for Level 3), or offer many reasons without explanations.

▲ **Excellent, 7–8-mark answers**
The best answers put forward many reasons and fully explain at least two of them. The main reason that better answers use is that conversion suggests that one religion is better than another, a suggestion that is against the idea of an equal, multi-faith society.

Summary

Multi-faith societies can cause issues for religions because:

• there may be **interfaith marriages**, which could cause tension between the two families

• children of these marriages may not know which religion to follow and that could cause problems within their families

• mixing up the religions could make everything very confusing and diluted.

4.10 Ways in which religions work to promote community cohesion in the UK

94

Learning outcomes

By the end of this lesson you should be able to:

- outline and explain the work religions do to promote community cohesion
- evaluate the role religions play in promoting community cohesion.

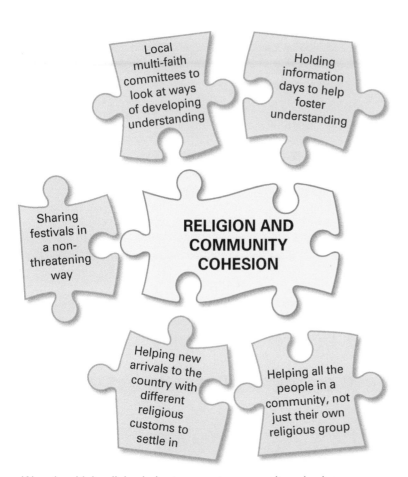

Local multi-faith committees to look at ways of developing understanding

Holding information days to help foster understanding

Sharing festivals in a non-threatening way

RELIGION AND COMMUNITY COHESION

Helping new arrivals to the country with different religious customs to settle in

Helping all the people in a community, not just their own religious group

Ways in which religion helps to promote community cohesion.

Activities

1 Try to find out what happens in your local area. Create a poster or leaflet that details any multi-faith events that are happening.

In Leeds headlines were made when a Muslim couple used a Christian church for their wedding.

Church wedding for Muslim couple

The Asian wedding guests entered the place of worship to cries of the Call to Prayer, a sound usually heard pouring from the doors of one of the city's mosques.

The bride, dressed in a traditional English white dress with veil, finally stepped out of her bridal car a good 15 minutes after the scheduled 10 a.m. service.

The bridegroom, who wore a white suit, waited at the altar.

The congregation listened as the reverend led the traditional English service, altered only in that prayers were directed to Allah and not God.

'Smile, relax and enjoy, make this your mosque today,' said the minister. 'Today is about bringing different faiths and creeds together, after all there is only one God although he might have many names.'

The Rev. Travis, who has been promoting interfaith religion for 25 years, told the *Yorkshire Evening Post* prior to the service: 'The bride and groom wanted a British wedding, but they are from a very traditional Muslim family. We will be having a very simple service, but you can imagine how difficult and uncomfortable this could be. The congregation is Muslim, there will be prayers from the Qur'an and we will address Allah, but this service will really help integrate the different faiths.'

Source: *The Yorkshire Evening Post*, 23.7.2007

What is the purpose of community cohesion?

Community cohesion is more than people just getting along together and tolerating each other. It is about understanding, caring and working together to improve the lives of the whole community.

The Inter Faith Network for the UK works both nationally and locally with different faith and educational communities to develop ideas and activities that promote community cohesion. (For more information, go to www.pearsonhotlinks. co.uk (express code 4226P) and click on the appropriate link.)

Faith schools

In England there are many faith schools that follow the national curriculum. There are Christian, Jewish and some Muslims schools. Some people think that faith schools create differences between children and prevent community cohesion.

In 2005 the Chief Inspector of Schools, David Bell wrote:

'*Many young people are being educated in faith-based schools, with little appreciation of their wider responsibilities and obligations to British society... we must not allow our recognition of diversity to become apathy in the face of any challenge to our coherence as a nation.*'

The Muslim Council of Britain represents Muslim groups all over Britain and aims to work for the good of society by encouraging Muslims to be part of the whole community and to create better relationships with other sectors of the community. It is possible to find small groups working all over the UK to promote community cohesion. Many of them have websites that advertise their activities: for an example go to www.pearsonhotlinks.co.uk (express code 4226P) and click on the WISE link. Below are some of the projects they have been involved in:

- building bridges initiative launched in 2006, with open days at the WISE Learning Centre and local media coverage
- visits to churches to build bridges and allay fears over media hype about Muslims
- WISE Youth Club started with outreach to young people of any faith
- involvement in the Wycombe Sharing of Faiths
- Muslim support to the Eden Chaplaincy service
- attendance at the Peace March, Faith Fayre and Dine at Mine initiatives
- involvement in police intiatives, e.g. Muslim Communication Forum
- school visits to talk to classes about different aspects of Islam.

Summary

- All religions want to live in peace.
- Local organisations are working together to establish strong multi-faith communities.

4.11 The media and community cohesion

> ## Learning outcomes
>
> By the end of this lesson you should be able to:
>
> - identify and describe how an issue from this section has been dealt with in the media
> - evaluate the treatment of the issue by the media
> - give your viewpoint with reasons about whether the issue was dealt with fairly.

A MUSLIM woman who said she was rejected for job in a trendy hair salon because she wore a headscarf has picked up £4,000 for her hurt 'feelings'.

Bushra Noah, 19, said salon owner Sarah Desrosiers religiously discriminated against her when she was turned down for a job.

But Ms Desrosiers said Ms Noah, of Acton, west London, was turned down because she needed stylists to reflect the 'funky, urban' image of her salon and showcase alternative hairstyles.

Yesterday the central London employment tribunal backed her complaint of indirect discrimination.

Ms Desrosiers, 32, said: 'I feel it is a bit steep for what actually happened. It's really scary for a small business.

'I never in a million years dreamt that somebody would be completely against the display of hair and be in this industry. I don't feel I deserve it.'

Ms Desrosiers added that if an applicant had a conventional hairstyle she would insist that it was re-styled in a more 'alternative' way.

The tribunal said that Ms Desrosiers and Ms Noah had a 15-minute interview last May at her Wedge salon in London's King's Cross.

But when the 19-year-old applicant arrived at the salon she claimed that the Canadian salon owner was clearly shocked by the fact she wore a headscarf.

Ms Desrosiers told the tribunal she was surprised that the younger woman had not mentioned it earlier.

Both parties told the tribunal it was obvious that the 19-year-old would not be offered the job.

But the tribunal panel awarded Ms Noah compensation as they concluded it was not known how her headscarf would affect the business.

The panel ruled: 'There was no specific evidence before us as to what would have been the actual impact of the claimant working in her salon with her head covered at all times.'

Article taken from the Sun *newspaper, June 2008.*

For discussion

What was your reaction when you read this story? Who did you think was right and who was wrong? Give reasons for your point of view.

How far do you think this story is fair to a religious person – e.g. the girl who would not remove her headscarf? Who do you think the reporter thought was right? How has this affected how the incident has been reported?

There are stories every day that claim to give unbiased reports about issues of community cohesion or racism. There are plays and soap opera storylines, as well as episodes of drama series, such as *The Bill*, that deal with these issues.

For example in the film *Bend It Like Beckham* an Asian Sikh family have difficulty coming to terms with the changing culture of Britain when they discover that their youngest daughter is brilliant at football. The story is about the clash between traditional values and the modern world.

The BBC 4 drama *White Girl* tells the story of a clash of cultures that occurs when a white family relocate from Leeds to an otherwise wholly Asian community in Bradford. Leah, the daughter, becomes friends with her neighbour Yasmin and discovers the culture that she thought was strange and frightening is not so alien after all. She is soon finding safety in the rituals of Islam away from the pain and strife at home.

Does it matter?

Everyone has the right to freedom of opinion and expression; this includes the right to hold opinions without interference and to seek, receive and impart information and ideas through any media regardless of frontiers.

Article 19 Universal Declaration of Human Rights

Many people think that the above declaration gives them the freedom to say what they like even if it offends others.

Activities

2 How far do you think we have the right to say what we like about religions or races? Do news reporters have a responsibility to encourage community cohesion? Collect some news stories that you think go too far along this idea and some stories that you think say the same thing without offence. Mount them for a display and under each one write your reasons for your choice.

Activities

1 Choose one form of the media: television, films, radio or the national press. Then choose one of the issues dealt with in this section of the book on religion and community cohesion.

   Devise some questions you might need to consider in order to evaluate how fair the story was to religious people when watching, listening to or reading about the issue.

   Compare notes with other students so that you have a comprehensive list of questions and then choose a story to evaluate.

Summary

- Issues of religion and community cohesion are part of everyday life and are often reported in the news or are part of a television storyline.
- Sometimes these stories are not fair to religious people.
- Everyone has a responsibility to ensure that people can live together in harmony.

Quick quiz

Complete the table below.

Key term	Definition
Community cohesion	
	Treating people less favourably because of their ethnicity/gender/colour/sexuality/age/class
Ethnic minority	
	Marriage where a husband and wife are from different religions
	Many different races and cultures living together in one society
Multi-faith society	
Prejudice	
Racial harmony	
	The belief that some races are superior to others
Religious freedom	
	Accepting all religions as having an equal right to exist
Sexism	

Student tips

When I studied these topics for my GCSE I made sure that I knew all the significant facts and understood all the main arguments for and against controversial issues. In this way, I could be sure of getting full marks for all the questions that asked for knowledge and understanding. For example, I could use my knowledge and understanding of the issues that cause racial tension to answer questions on the causes and possible solutions to such problems.

Self-evaluation checklist

Read through the following list and evaluate how well you know and understand each of the topics.
How well have you understood the topics in this section? In the first column of the table below use the following code to rate your understanding:

Green – I understand this fully.

Orange – I am confident I can answer most questions on this.

Red – I need to do a lot more work on this topic.

In the second and third columns you need to think about:

● Whether you have an opinion on this topic and could give reasons for that opinion, if asked.

● Whether you can give the opinion of someone who disagrees with you and give reasons for this alternative opinion.

Content covered	My understanding is red/orange/green	Can I give my opinion?	Can I give an alternative opinion?
● Outline changing attitudes towards gender roles in the UK.			
● Explain and evaluate Muslim attitudes towards equal rights for women in religion.			
● Understand how the UK works as a multi-ethnic society, and how the government works to promote community cohesion.			
● Outline the work of a Muslim organisation to help asylum seekers.			
● Explain why Muslims should promote racial harmony.			
● Outline and explain Muslim attitudes to other religions.			
● Describe ways in which religions work to promote community cohesion.			

examzone

KnowZone
Religion and community cohesion

Introduction

In the exam you will see a choice of two questions on this section. Each question will include four tasks, which test your knowledge, understanding and evaluation of the material covered. A 2-mark question will ask you to define a term; a 4-mark question will ask your opinion on a point of view; an 8-mark question will ask you to explain a particular belief or idea;

a 6-mark question will ask for your opinion on a point of view and ask you to consider an alternative point of view.

Choose the question you can answer best – remembering you need to answer all parts of the question you choose!

Mini exam paper

(a) What is a **multi-ethnic society**? (2 marks)

(b) Do you think that women should have equal rights in religion?

Give **two** reasons for your point of view. (4 marks)

(c) Explain why interfaith marriages can cause problems for religious families. (8 marks)

(d) 'If everyone were religious, there would be no racism.'

In your answer you should refer to Islam.

   (i) Do you agree? Give reasons for your opinion. (3 marks)

   (ii) Give reasons why some people may disagree with you. (3 marks)

Here you need to give a short, accurate definition. You do not need to write more than one clear sentence.

You must give your opinion, but make sure you do give two clear and properly thought-out reasons. These can be ones you have learned in class, even if they are not your own opinion. You mustn't use terms such as 'rubbish' or 'stupid' as these don't show that you are able to think things through carefully.

The word 'explain' means you should give details of activities religious families may carry out together or ways in which they share their faith, but you must also show how these may lead to belief in Allah. This question is worth 8 marks so you must be prepared to spend some time answering it. You will also be assessed on your use of language in this question.

In your answer you should state whether or not you agree with the statement. You should also give reasons for your opinion.

In either (i) or (ii) you must refer to Islam.

Now you have to give the opposite point of view, again using material you have learned during your studies. You don't have to say what you think about these alternative points of view, but you do need to show you understand why they are just as important to consider as your own opinion.

Mark scheme

(a) You can earn **2 marks** for a correct answer, and **1 mark** for a partially correct answer.

(b) To earn up to the full **4 marks** you need to give two reasons and develop them. Two brief reasons or only one developed reason will earn **2 marks**.

(c) You can earn **7–8 marks** by giving up to four reasons, but the fewer reasons you give, the more you must develop them. Because you are being assessed on use of language, you also need to take care to express your understanding in a clear style of English, and make some use of specialist vocabulary.

(d) To go beyond **3 marks** for the whole of this question you must refer to at least one religion. The more you are able to develop your reasons the more marks you will earn. Three simple reasons can earn you the same mark as one fully developed reason.

ResultsPlus
Build Better Answers

(c) Explain why mixed-faith marriages may cause problems for religious families. (8 marks)

Student answer	Comments	Improved student answer
Mixed-faith marriages cause problems for religious families because the family may feel that their religion is right and the other religion is wrong. Also, they may feel that if their son or daughter is getting married, then they will have to change their religious faith and join a religion whose teachings they do not believe in.	The student gives two good reasons here but does not develop them fully. They would need to do this to improve their answer. Alternatively they could add two more reasons.	Mixed-faith marriages cause problems for religious families because the family may feel that their religion is right and the other religion is wrong. This might cause conflict and arguments about different issues. Also, they may feel that if their son or daughter is getting married, then they will have to change their religious faith and join a religion whose teachings they do not believe in. If the couple have children then there may also be conflict about how they are brought up – which religion should they follow? A child might be confused by this.

Welcome to examzone

Revising for your exams can be a daunting prospect. In this part of the book we'll take you through the best way of revising for your exams, step by step, to ensure you perform as well as you can.

Zone In!

Have you ever become so absorbed in a task that suddenly it feels entirely natural and easy to perform? This is a feeling familiar to many athletes and performers. They work hard to recreate it in competition in order to do their very best. It's a feeling of being 'in the zone', and if you can achieve that same feeling in an examination, the chances are you'll perform brilliantly.

The good news is that you can get 'in the zone' by taking some simple steps in advance of the exam. Here are our top tips.

UNDERSTAND IT

Make sure you understand the exam process and what revision you need to do. This will give you confidence and also help you to get things into proportion. These pages are a good place to find some starting pointers for performing well in exams.

FRIENDS AND FAMILY

Make sure that your friends and family know when you want to revise. Even share your revision plan with them. Learn to control your times with them, so you don't get distracted. This means you can have better quality time with them when you aren't revising, because you aren't worrying about what you ought to be doing.

DEAL WITH DISTRACTIONS

Think about the issues in your life that may interfere with revision. Write them all down. Then think about how you can deal with each so they don't affect your revision.

COMPARTMENTALISE

You might not be able to deal with all the issues that can distract you. For example, you may be worried about a friend who is ill, or just be afraid of the exam. In this case, there is still a useful technique you can use. Put all of these worries into an imagined box in your mind at the start of your revision (or in the exam) and mentally lock it. Only open it again at the end of your revision session (or exam).

DIET AND EXERCISE

Make sure you eat sensibly and exercise as well! If your body is not in the right state, how can your mind be? A substantial breakfast will set you up for the day, and a light evening meal will keep your energy levels high.

BUILD CONFIDENCE

Use your revision time not only to revise content, but also to build your confidence in readiness for tackling the examination. For example, try tackling a short sequence of easy tasks in record time.

Planning Zone

The key to success in exams and revision often lies in good planning. Knowing **what** you need to do and **when** you need to do it is your best path to a stress-free experience. Here are some top tips in creating a great personal revision plan.

First of all, *know your strengths and weaknesses.*

Go through each topic making a list of how well you think you know the topic. Use your mock examination results and/or any other test results that are available as a check on your self-assessment. This will help you to plan your personal revision effectively, putting extra time into your weaker areas.

Next, *create your plan!*

Remember to make time for considering how topics interrelate.

For example, in PE you will be expected to know not just about the various muscles, but how these relate to various body types.

The specification quite clearly states when you are expected to be able to link one topic to another so plan this into your revision sessions.

You will be tested on this in the exam and you can improve your answers by showing your ability to do this.

Finally, *follow the plan!*

You can use the revision sections in the following pages to kick-start your revision.

103

MAY

SUNDAY	MONDAY	TUE
30	1
7	8
13
20	22
27	28

30
Be realistic about how much time you can devote to your revision, but also make sure you put in enough time. Give yourself regular breaks or different activities to give your life some variance. Revision need not be a prison sentence!

1
Find out your exam dates. Go to the Edexcel website www.edexcel.com to find all final exam dates, and check with your teacher.

View Sect
complete
ractice e
questio

7
Chunk your revision in each subject down into smaller sections. This will make it more manageable and less daunting.

8
Draw up a list of all the dates from the start of your revision right through to your exams.

Review Sectio
Complete three
practice exam

Make sure you allow time for assessing your progress against your initial self-assessment. Measuring progress will allow you to see and be encouraged by your improvement. These little victories will build your confidence.

20
Review Sectio
Try the Keywor
Quiz again

22
EXAM DAY!

KnowZone
Section 1: Believing in Allah

In this section, you need to show the examiner not only that you know about issues relating to belief in Allah (AO1), but that you understand why some Muslims differ in the beliefs they hold (AO2).

This is an important skill to demonstrate, but not an easy one. It means that you have to have learned the facts first – for example, what it means to say that Allah is omni-benevolent. Some may believe this means we should expect Allah to perform miracles, while others may believe it means Allah should answer prayer. Other Muslims may argue that Allah doesn't *have* to do either of these things, but that when he doesn't people should not think this means he isn't loving.

Muslims have a number of responses to the problem of evil and suffering. All believe that because Allah is omnipotent, omniscient and omni-benevolent, he is in control. You need to show that not only do you understand how this belief affects Muslim ideas about why people suffer, but you must also be able to explain what they base their ideas on, e.g. the teaching in the Qur'an and the Hadith.

As part of the AO2 assessment you also have to be able to explain your own views and assess why and how they differ from other possible views. The issue here is that you can be critical of your own views as well as those of others and recognise the variety of beliefs that can be held.

Revision

Look back at the KnowZone that appears at the end of the section, on pages 22–25. Read through the self-evaluation checklist and think about which are your stronger and weaker areas, so that you can focus on the ones you are less confident about. You may like to try the Quick quiz again, the Plenary activity, or the Support activity below.

When you are ready for some exam practice, read through the KnowZone on pages 24–25. Then you might like to attempt the questions on the right.

Support activity

Question (d) about religious broadcasting on television needs to be based on real evidence of television programmes on religious themes, so make sure you have some at hand to refer to. Pick any suitable programme and watch it as part of your revision. Jot down some notes either while you are watching or just after. You may like to consider these quotes and whether the programme supports or does not support the views:

'Religious programmes on television are usually supportive of religious believers.'

'Religious programmes on television say more about reasons not to believe in Allah than to believe in him.'

'Television programmes about religious beliefs discourage people from believing in Allah.'

Practice exam questions

(a) What is meant by **numinous**? (2 marks)

(b) Do you think Allah is the cause of the universe?

Give **two** reasons for your point of view. (4 marks)

(c) Explain how Muslims respond to the problem of evil and suffering. (8 marks)

(d) 'Religious programmes on television or the radio, or films, encourage you to believe in Allah.'

In your answer you should refer to Islam.

(i) Do you agree? Give reasons for your opinion. (3 marks)

(ii) Give reasons why some people may disagree with you. (3 marks)

Section 2: Matters of life and death

The material in this section tends to deal with issues that are not just of concern to religious people, but to everyone. We all care about matters of life and death, not least because we will all die! But, until we do, we want to be sure that our life and the lives of others, whether they are close to us or not, are treated with respect.

In this section, it is important that you ensure you gain marks from considering the particular concerns of Muslims, even though they may be quite different from your own. Some of these concerns may also be shared by some non-religious believers. Make sure you understand what makes these views distinctive to Muslims. For example, issues such as the sanctity of life and the belief that Allah created human beings for a special purpose are likely to form part of the Muslim position on matters of life and death. So, a Muslim might say this is the reason they are against euthanasia; but a non-religious person might also be against it, because they think it is always more important to preserve life than take it away.

Revision

Look back at the KnowZone that appears at the end of the section, on pages 46–49. Read through the Self-evaluation checklist and think about which are your stronger and weaker areas, so that you can focus on the ones you are less confident about. You may like to try the Quick quiz again, the Plenary activity, or the Support activity below.

When you are ready for some exam practice, read through the KnowZone on pages 48–49. Then you might like to attempt the questions on the right.

Support activity

Question (d) is about the paranormal. It is probably one of the trickier questions you can get, as it really is a matter of opinion. No one can actually prove whether paranormal activity is genuine or not. Your understanding of this area would be helped by finding out, as a class or in small groups, about some popular views on the paranormal. Find out about television shows and so-called 'celebrity' mediums such as Tony Stockwell. They have an enormous following. Discuss why you think this is the case, and if that in any way proves they are genuinely in touch with the paranormal.

Practice exam questions

(a) What is **resurrection**? (2 marks)

(b) Do you agree with abortion?

Give **two** reasons for your point of view. (4 marks)

(c) Explain why most Muslims are against euthanasia. (8 marks)

(d) 'The paranormal proves that there is life after death.'

In your answer you should refer to Islam.

(i) Do you agree? Give reasons for your opinion. (3 marks)

(ii) Give reasons why some people may disagree with you. (3 marks)

KnowZone
Section 3: Marriage and the family

Obtaining good AO2 answers in this section depends on your being able to distinguish between genuine difference of opinion on the one hand and prejudice or ignorance on the other.

For example, Muslims may have a range of views on homosexuality – those views will be supported by what they hold to be a genuine interpretation of sacred texts or other valid religious teachings. Even if you don't agree with them, in most cases they will be held for good reasons, not just out of prejudice for or against homosexual people. Remember, too, not to assume that all religious people are against everything! Many religious believers today adopt a liberal approach to a lot of these issues, and you need to show that you understand why that is the case.

Revision

Look back at the KnowZone that appears at the end of the section, on pages 70–73. Read through the Self-evaluation checklist and think about which are your stronger and weaker areas, so that you can focus on the ones you are less confident about. You may like to try the Quick quiz again, the Plenary activity, or the Support activity below.

When you are ready for some exam practice, read through the KnowZone on pages 72–73. Then you might like to attempt the questions on the right.

Support activity

Question (b) on contraception asks for your opinion without specifying that you refer to Islam. It is a question that need not have anything to do with religion, but at the same time you need to show that you do understand Muslim views and that they might be held for special reasons. As a group or in pairs compare the attitudes towards contraception shown in the two contrasting websites for pregnancy advice and contraception. These can be accessed on our hotlinks website, www.pearsonhotlinks.co.uk (express code 4226P).

What do they tell you about how believers and non-believers feel about contraception? What audiences do you think they are aimed at? Are they persuasive websites? (This means: do they convey their messages in a way that would encourage people to adopt their views?)

Practice exam questions

(a) What is a **nuclear family?** (2 marks)

(b) Do you think it is right to use contraception?

Give **two** reasons for your point of view. (4 marks)

(c) Explain why there are different attitudes to divorce in Islam. (8 marks)

(d) 'A religious family is a happy family.'

In your answer you should refer to Islam.

(i) Do you agree? Give reasons for your opinion. (3 marks)

(ii) Give reasons why some people may disagree with you. (3 marks)

Similarly to matters of life and death, the issues you study in community cohesion are ones of general concern, not just of concern to Muslims. Your task in the exam is to show that you understand both how Muslims tackle these issues and the beliefs that underlie their attitudes to matters of community cohesion.

These issues are important for society as well as for religion, but you need to distinguish between these in the exam. For example, a question that asks you if you agree that there should be equal rights for women in religion demands a different response from you than if the question asked whether women should have equal rights in society.

In question (d) in this section, make sure that you do not express any personal feelings that may appear to be unsympathetic to community cohesion. This is not an appropriate response for an examination, where you need to deal with matters in an academic way.

Revision

Look back at the KnowZone that appears at the end of the section, on pages 98–101. Read through the Self-evaluation checklist and think about which are your stronger and weaker areas, so that you can focus on the ones you are less confident about. You may like to try the Quick quiz again, the Plenary activity, or the Support activity below.

When you are ready for some exam practice, read through the KnowZone on pages 100–101. Then you might like to attempt the questions on the right.

Support activity

To help you answer question (b) about whether religious believers have the right to convert you, discuss as a group any experience you have had of either trying to convert others to your faith or when someone tried to convert you. Listen carefully to each other's views and don't make any judgements. Instead, after you've shared any experiences of this, make a list of the feelings that you think people from each group may have had. For example, feelings of rejection, anger and bewilderment may all be relevant, but also feelings of encouragement, well-being or comfort.

Practice exam questions

(a) What is **racism**? (2 marks)

(b) Do people from a different religion have the right to try to convert you?

Give **two** reasons for your point of view. (4 marks)

(c) Explain why Muslims should work to promote racial harmony. (8 marks)

(d) 'Islam needs women teachers.'
In your answer you should refer to Islam.

(i) Do you agree? Give reasons for your opinion. (3 marks)

(ii) Give reasons why some people may disagree with you. (3 marks)

108

Don't Panic Zone

As you get close to completing your revision, the Big Day will be getting nearer and nearer. Many students find this the most stressful time and tend to go into panic mode, either working long hours without really giving their brains a chance to absorb information, or giving up and staring blankly at the wall.

Panicking simply makes your brain seize up and you find that information and thoughts simply cannot flow naturally. You become distracted and anxious, and things seem worse than they are. Many students build the exams up into more than they are. Remember: the exams are not trying to catch you out! If you have studied the course, there will be no surprises on the exam paper!

Student tips

I know how silly it is to panic, especially if you've done the work and know your stuff. I was asked by a teacher to produce a report on a project I'd done, and I panicked so much I spent the whole afternoon crying and worrying. I asked other people for help, but they were panicking too. In the end, I calmed down and looked at the task again. It turned out to be quite straightforward and, in the end, I got my report finished first and it was the best of them all!

In the exam you don't have much time, so you can't waste it by panicking. The best way to control panic is simply to do what you have to do. Think carefully for a few minutes, then start writing and as you do, the panic will drain away.

Don't panic

ExamZone

If you are sitting your exams from 2014 onwards, you will be sitting all your exams together at the end of your course. Make sure you know in which order you are sitting the exams, and prepare for each accordingly – check with your teacher if you're not sure. They are likely to be about a week apart, so make sure you allow plenty of revision time for each before your first exam.

You will have one and a half hours for this exam paper and in that time you have to answer **four** questions, one on each of the four sections you have studied: Believing in Allah, Matters of life and death, Marriage and the family and Religion and community cohesion.

In each section, you can make a choice from two questions.

Each question will be made up of four different parts:

- a 2-mark question will ask for you to define a term
- a 4-mark question will ask for your opinion on a point of view
- an 8-mark question will ask you to explain a particular belief or idea
- a 6-mark question will ask for your opinion on a point of view and ask you to consider an alternative point of view.

Effectively you shouldn't spend more than 22.5 minutes on each section (that's 90 minutes divided by 4):

- the 8-mark question deserves the most attention, so that's around 9 minutes
- the 2-mark question should take you 1.5 minutes, then
- 5 minutes for the 4-mark question, and
- the remaining 7 minutes for the 6-mark question.

Obviously you can give or take here or there, and your teacher may guide you differently, but as long as you don't go over 22.5 minutes altogether and the length of each of your answers is appropriate for the number of marks available, then you'll be on the right lines.

Meet the exam paper

This diagram shows the front cover of the exam paper. These instructions, information and advice will always appear on the front of the paper. It is worth reading it carefully now. Check you understand it. Now is a good opportunity to ask your teacher about anything you are not sure of here.

Print your surname here, and your other names afterwards to ensure that the exam board awards the marks to the right candidate.

Here you fill in the school's exam number.

Ensure that you understand exactly how long the examination will last, and plan your time accordingly.

Note that the quality of your written communication will also be marked. Take particular care to present your thoughts and work at the highest standard you can. If extra marks are awarded for your spelling, punctuation and grammar it will be highlighted on the front page of your exam paper, and by an asterisk next to the questions affected.

Here you fill in your personal exam number. Take care when writing it down because the number is important to the exam board when writing your score.

In this box, the examiner will write the total marks you have achieved in the exam paper.

Make sure that you understand exactly which questions from which sections you should attempt.

Don't feel that you have to fill the answer space provided. Everybody's handwriting varies, so a long answer from you may take up as much space as a short answer from someone else.

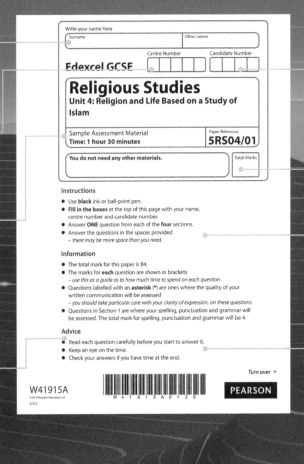

Practical tips on the exam paper

- You must use a black pen. Your paper is scanned into a computer for marking. If you write in any other colour, you risk your work not being seen clearly.

- You must choose your question carefully – cross out the one you are not going to do – to avoid changing a question half-way through answering it. This is a very common mistake and costs candidates lots of marks!

- Mark with an x at the top of the page which question you have chosen.

- Do not write outside the guidelines – your answer may get cut off by the scanning process.

- Do not use extra sheets and attach them unless it is absolutely necessary. If you need more space – for example, for a (b) question – continue into the (c) space and when you change question write your own (c). Do the same for (c) into (d). If you then run out, put an arrow and write at the end of the exam booklet.

This section provides answers to the most common questions students have about what happens after they complete their exams. For more information, visit www.pearsonhotlinks.co.uk (express code 4226P) and click on ExamZone.

About your grades

Whether you've done better than, worse than, or just as you expected, your grades are the final measure of your performance on your course and in the exams. On this page we explain some of the information that appears on your results slip and tell you what to do if you think something is wrong. We answer the most popular questions about grades and look at some of the options facing you.

When will my results be published?

Results for GCSE summer examinations are issued on the third Thursday in August. January exam results are issued in March and March exam results issued in April.

If you are sitting your exams from 2014 onwards, there will no longer be January sittings: you will sit all of your exams in June.

Can I get my results online?

Visit www.pearsonhotlinks.co.uk (express code 4226P) and click on Results Plus, where you will find detailed student results information including the 'Edexcel Gradeometer' which demonstrates how close you were to the nearest grade boundary.

I haven't done as well as I expected. What can I do now?

First of all, talk to your subject teacher. After all the teaching, tests and internal examinations that you have had, he/she is the person who best knows what grade you are capable of achieving. Take your results slip to your subject teacher, and go through the information on it in detail. If you both think there is something wrong with the result, the school or college can apply to see your completed examination paper and then, if necessary, ask for a re-mark immediately. Bear in mind that the original mark can be confirmed or lowered, as well as raised, as a result of a re-mark.

How do my grades compare with those of everybody else who sat this exam?

You can compare your results with those of others in the UK who have completed the same examination using the information on the Edexcel website accessed at www.pearsonhotlinks.co.uk (express code 4226P) by clicking on Edexcel.

What happens if I was ill over the period of my examinations?

If you become ill before or during the examination period you are eligible for special consideration. This also applies if you have been affected by an accident, bereavement or serious disturbance during an examination.

If my school has requested special consideration for me, is this shown on my Statement of Results?

If your school has requested special consideration for you, it is not shown on your results slip, but it will be shown on a subject mark report that is sent to your school or college. If you want to know whether special consideration was requested for you, you should ask your Examinations Officer.

Can I have a re-mark of my examination paper?

Yes, this is possible, but remember that only your school or college can apply for a re-mark, not you or your parents/carers. First of all, you should consider carefully whether or not to ask your school or college to make a request for a re-mark. It is worth knowing that very few re-marks result in a change to a grade – not because Edexcel is embarrassed that a change of marks has been made, but simply because a re-mark request has shown that the original marking was accurate. Check the closing date for re-marking requests with your Examinations Officer.

When I asked for a re-mark of my paper, my subject grade went down. What can I do?

There is no guarantee that your grades will go up if your papers are re-marked. They can also go down or stay the same. After a re-mark, the only way to improve your grade is to take the examination again. Your school or college Examinations Officer can tell you when you can do that.

Can I resit this unit?

If you are sitting your exams before 2014, you may resit a unit once prior to claiming certification for the qualification. If you are sitting your exams from 2014 onwards, you will not be able to resit any of the exams.

For much more information, go to www.pearsonhotlinks.co.uk (express code 4226P) and click on examzone.

Glossary

Abortion – The removal of an embryo or foetus from the womb before it can survive

Adultery – A sexual act between a married person and someone other than their marriage partner

Agnosticism – Not being sure whether Allah exists

Akhirah – Muslim beliefs about life after death

Al'Jannah – Heaven or Paradise (literally the garden)

Aqiqa – Muslim naming ceremony, when a baby's hair is shaved and its weight in gold or silver is given to charity

Assisted suicide – Providing a seriously ill person with the means to commit suicide

Asylum seeker – Someone who looks for protection and shelter in another country

Atheism – Believing that Allah does not exist

Barzakh – The time between death and the Last Day

Bismillah – The ceremony in some cultures when a Muslim child formally begins to learn about Islam

Civil partnership – A legal ceremony giving a homosexual couple the same legal rights as a husband and wife

Cohabitation – Living together without being married

Community cohesion – A common vision and shared sense of belonging for all groups in society

Contraception – Intentionally preventing pregnancy from occurring

Contract – The legal document of marriage

Conversion – When your life is changed by giving yourself to Allah

Discrimination – Treating people less favourably because of their ethnicity/gender/colour/sexuality/age/class

Divorce – The legal termination of a marriage

Embryo – The developing human during the first eight weeks after conception

Equality – The state of everyone having equal rights regardless of their gender, race or class

Ethnic minority – A member of an ethnic group (race) which is much smaller than the majority group

Euthanasia – The painless killing of someone dying from a painful disease

Extended family – Where parents, children and other relations such as grandparents, aunts, uncles and cousins all live close together

Foetus – The developing human from day 57 after conception to birth

Free will – The idea that human beings are free to make their own choices

Gender – Sex, being male or female

Hadith – Sayings and actions of the prophet Muhammad as recorded by his family and friends

Halal – That which is permitted or lawful

Hajj – Fifth pillar of Islam, pilgrimage to Makkah

Homosexuality – Sexual attraction to the same sex

Imam – A prayer leader. Guides and teaches about Islam

Interfaith marriage – Marriage where the husband and wife are from different religions

Iqamah – The call to stand up for prayer

LEDC – Less economically developed country

Madrassah – Muslim school based at the mosque

Mahr – A sum of money placed in trust for a bride by her husband at the wedding

Marriage – Where a man and woman are legally united for the purpose of living together as a couple

Mediums – People who claim to be able to contact the dead

Miracle – Something which seems to break a law of science and makes you think only Allah could have done it

Moral evil – Actions done by humans which cause suffering

Mosque – Place for communal prayer and activities

Multi-ethnic society – Many different races and cultures living together in one society

Multi-faith society – Many different religions living together in one society

Natural evil – Things which cause suffering but have nothing to do with humans

Nikah – The signing of the marriage contract

Non-voluntary euthanasia – Ending someone's life painlessly when they are unable to ask, but you have good reason for thinking they would want you to do so

Nuclear family – Mother, father and children living as a unit

Numinous – The feeling of the presence of something greater than you

Omni-benevolent – The belief that Allah is all-good

Omnipotent – The belief that Allah is all-powerful

Omniscient – The belief that Allah knows everything that has happened and everything that is going to happen

Paranormal – Unexplained things which are thought to have spiritual causes eg ghosts, mediums

People of the Book – The name for Jews and Christians in the Qur'an

Prayer – An attempt to contact Allah, usually through words

Prejudice – Believing some people are inferior or superior without even knowing them

Pre-marital sex – Sex before marriage

Procreation – Making a new life

Promiscuity – Having sex with a number of partners without commitment

Quality of life – The idea that life must have some benefits for it to be worth living

Racial harmony – Different races/colours living together happily

Racism – The belief that some races are superior to others

Re-constituted family – Where two sets of children (stepbrothers and stepsisters) become one family when their divorced parents marry each other

Reincarnation – The belief that, after death, souls are reborn into another body

Religious freedom – The right to practise your religion and change your religion

Religious pluralism – Accepting all religions as having an equal right to coexist

Resurrection – The belief that, after death, the body stays in the grave until the end of the world when it is raised

Sacrament – Used by some people to mean a special agreement between God and man

Sadaqah – Voluntary charitable giving

Salah – One of the five pillars of Islam. The five daily prayers

Same-sex family – Two same-sex parents and their children

Sanctity of life – The belief that life is holy and belongs to Allah

Sexism – Discriminating against people because of their gender (being male or female)

Single-parent family – One parent living alone with their children as a result of divorce, separation, death or because the parent is unmarried

Ummah – The worldwide Muslim community

Unbiased – A fair approach to an issue; not affected by prejudice

Voluntary euthanasia – Ending life painlessly when someone in great pain asks for death

Walimah – Celebration of the marriage

Zakah – Charitable tax given by all Muslims once a year

Index

Key terms from the beginning of each topic are shown as main entries in bold type, and the page number that is also in bold will take you to a definition of the word.